Humanity, Belief, and Islam

1-9 Words - The Eleventh Word -

The Twenty-first Word

Bediüzzaman
Said Nursi

Rutherford, New Jersey
2002

Copyright © 2002 by The Light, Inc.
&
Copyright © 2002 by Işık Yayınları

All rights reserved. No part of this book may be reproduced or transmitted in any form or by any means, electronic or mechanical, including photocopying, recording or by any information storage and retrieval system without permission in writing from the Publisher.

Published by The Light, Inc.

42 Park Ave.

Rutherford, NJ 07070 USA

www.thelightinc.com

contact@thelightinc.com

Library of Congress Cataloging-in-Publication
data available

Nursi, Said, 1873-1960.
Humanity, Belief, and Islam /
Bediuzzaman Said Nursi.
p. cm. -- (From the Risale-i nur collection)
Includes index.
ISBN 0-9720654-6-6 (pbk.)

Printed and bound in Turkey

Table of Contents

Bediüzzaman and the Risale-i Nur ii
Humanity, Belief, and Islam 1
  Introduction 2

THE FIRST WORD
The Worth of *Bismillah* 3

THE SECOND WORD
The Way to Contentment 25

THE THIRD WORD
Choosing the Right Way 29

THE FOURTH WORD
The Prescribed Prayers' Value 33

THE FIFTH WORD
The Right Training for Believers 36

THE SIXTH WORD
The Supreme Transaction 40

THE SEVENTH WORD
The Door to Human Happiness 49

THE EIGHTH WORD
The Necessity of Religion 57

THE NINTH WORD
The Different Prayer Times 66

THE ELEVENTH WORD
Creation and Prayer 81

THE TWENTY-FIRST WORD
The Prayer 99
Index 109

Bediüzzaman and the Risale-i Nur

In the many dimensions of his lifetime of achievement, as well as in his personality and character, Bediüzzaman (1873-1960) was and, through his continuing influence, still is an important thinker and writer in the Muslim world. He represented in a most effective and profound way the intellectual, moral and spiritual strengths of Islam, evident in different degrees throughout its fourteen-century history. He lived for eighty-five years. He spent almost all of those years, overflowing with love and ardor for the cause of Islam, in a wise and measured activism based on sound reasoning and in the shade of the Qur'an and the Prophetic example.

Bediüzzaman lived in an age when materialism was at its peak and many crazed after communism, and the world was in great crisis. In that critical period, Bediüzzaman pointed people to the source of belief and inculcated in them a strong hope for a collective restoration. At a time when science and philosophy were used to mislead young generations into atheism, and nihilistic attitudes had a wide appeal, at a time when all this was done in the name of civilization, modernization and contemporary thinking and those who tried to resist them were subjected to the cruelest of persecutions, Bediüzzaman strove for the overall revival of a whole people, breathing into their minds whatever and spirits whatever is taught in the institutions of both modern and traditional education and of spiritual training.

Bediüzzaman had seen that modern unbelief originated from science and philosophy, not from ignorance as previously. He wrote that nature is the collection of Divine signs and therefore science and religion cannot be conflicting disciplines. Rather, they are two (apparently) different expressions of the same truth. Minds should be enlightened with sciences, while hearts need to be illumined by religion.

Bediüzzaman was not a writer in the usual sense of the word. He wrote his splendid work the *Risale-i Nur*, a collection exceeding 5,000 pages, because he had a mission: he struggled against the materialistic and atheistic trends of thought fed by science and philosophy and tried to present the truths of Islam to modern minds and hearts of every level of understanding. The *Risale-i Nur*, a modern commentary of the Qur'an, mainly concentrates on the existence and unity of God, the Resurrection, Prophethood, the Divine Scriptures primarily including the Qur'an, the invisible realms of existence, Divine Destiny and humanity's free will, worship, justice in human life, and humanity's place and duty among the creation.

In order to remove from people's minds and hearts the accumulated 'sediment' of false beliefs and conceptions and to purify them both intellectually and spiritually, Bediüzzaman writes forcefully and makes reiterations. He writes in neither an academic nor a didactic way; rather he appeals to feelings and aims to pour out his thoughts and ideas into people's hearts and minds in order to awaken them to belief and conviction.

This book is a selected section from the *Risale-i Nur* collection.

Humanity, Belief, and Islam

> In the Name of God,
> the Merciful, the Compassionate.

> And from Him do we seek help. Praise be to God, the Lord of all worlds, and blessings and peace be upon our master Muhammad,[1] his Family,[2] and his Companions.

Introduction

---

[1] In any publication dealing with Prophet Muhammad, his name or title is followed by "upon him be peace and blessings," to show our respect for him and because it is a religious requirement to do so. For his Companions and other illustrious Muslims of the past: "May God be pleased with him (or her)" is used. However, as this might be distracting to non-Muslim readers, these phrases do not appear in this book, on the understanding that they are assumed and that no disrespect is intended. (Ed.)

[2] The Prophet's Family: The Prophet, Ali, Fatima, Hasan, and Husayn. These people are known as the *Ahl al-Bayt,* the Family (or People) of the House. The Prophet's wives are not included in this designation. (Tr.)

Fellow Muslims. You asked for advice, so listen to a few truths contained in the following allegories. Since you are soldiers, I will express them in military terms.

THE FIRST WORD

The Worth of *Bismillah*

Bismillah (In the Name of God) is the start of all good things, so we shall start with it. This blessed phrase is a mark of Islam, one constantly recited by all creatures through their tongues of disposition. If you want to perceive its inexhaustible source of strength and blessing, consider the following allegory:

Travelers in Arabian deserts must travel under a tribal chief's name and protection, or else they will be bothered by bandits and unable to acquire what they need for the journey. Two people,[3] one humble and the other arrogant, set

---

[3] The Qur'an declares: *I shall not allow to go to waste the deed of any doer among you, whether be a male or female: you are one from the other* (3:195). It is clear that Islam does not discriminate between men and women in religious responsibility. Each gender shares most of the responsibilities, but each one has certain responsibilities that are particular to it. The Qur'an usually uses the mas-

out on a journey. The humble one obtained the name of a tribal chief; the arrogant one did not. The former traveled everywhere in safety. Whenever he met a bandit, he said: "I'm travelling in the name of this chief," and so was left alone. He was treated with respect in every tent he entered. In contrast, the arrogant one suffered disaster and constant fear, for he had to struggle and beg for every need. He became base and vile.

O arrogant soul! You are that traveler, and this world is the desert. Your weakness and poverty are endless, and the enemies and privations to which you are exposed are beyond number. Given this, invoke the name of the Eternal Owner and the Everlasting Ruler of this world,

---

culine form of address, for this is one of Arabic's characteristics. In almost every language, the masculine form is used for a group comprising both men and women, like the English word *mankind*, which includes both men and women. So, brotherhood also includes sisterhood, and, since the believers comprise both male and female believers, the believers are bothers and sisters. However, in order to maintain the original text and avoid repetition, usually we do not mention the feminine forms in translation. (Tr.)

for only this can deliver you from such begging and fear.

Bismillah is a blessed treasure. It transforms your boundless weakness and poverty, by binding you to the Omnipotent and Merciful One's infinite Power and Mercy, into the most heeded intercessor at His Exalted Court. When you say *bismillah*, you act in His name. You are like a soldier acting in the state's name, fearing no one, doing all things in the name of the law and the state, and persisting against all odds.

How does everything recite *bismillah* via its very mode of existence? For example: A stranger arriving in a city can order its people to gather at a certain place to work on a certain task. If this order is obeyed, the stranger obviously is acting in the name of the ruler's strength and authority, not his own. In the same way, everything acts in the name of God, the All-Mighty. Small seeds and grains carry huge trees on their heads and raise weights as heavy as mountains. Each tree says *bismillah* and, filling its hands with fruit from Mercy's treasury, offers them to us on a tray. Each garden, a cooking pot from the Divine Power's kitchen where countless varieties of delicious foods are prepared, says *bismillah*.

All blessed animals (e.g., cows, camels, sheep, and goats) say *bismillah* and become fountains of milk from Mercy's abundance. They offer us, in the Provider's name, a most delicate and pure food like the water of life. Every plant and blade of grass, every root and stem, says *bismillah*. All plant, tree, and grass roots and fibers, soft as silk, say *bismillah* and pierce hard stones and soil. Mentioning His Name, the Name of the Merciful, subjects everything to them.

A tree's branches spread in the sky, and its roots spread unhindered among stones and soil. It generates underground spontaneously, and its delicate green leaves hold moisture despite intense heat. These realities vex the naturalist. It jabs a finger into the naturalist's unseeing eye and says: "You put so much trust in the power of hardness and heat, yet they obey the Divine Command.

That is why each soft fiber of the plant's roots, like Moses' staff, obeys: *And We said: "O Moses, strike the rock with your staff"* (2:60) and penetrates the rock. Every delicate, paper-thin leaf, like one of Abraham's limbs, recites: *O fire, be coolness and peace* (21:69) in defiance of the intense heat.

All things inwardly say *bismillah* and deliver God's bounties to us in His name. Thus we also should say *bismillah*, give and take in His name, and accept nothing from those who do not give in God's name.

QUESTION: We pay people for whatever they bring us, even though they are only "tray-bearers." What payment does God, their true Owner, ask of us?

ANSWER: That true Bestower of all precious bounties and goods we enjoy requires three things: remembrance, thanksgiving, and reflection. Saying *bismillah* at the beginning is a manner of remembrance, and saying *al-hamdu lillah* (praise and thanks be to God) at their end is a manner of thanksgiving. Reflection means always being mindful and thinking of the precious and ingenious bounties we receive as miracles of the Eternally-Besought-of-All's Power and as gifts from His Mercy.

If you kissed the hand of someone who brought you a precious gift without recognizing the true sender (the king), you would be making a great mistake. Praising and loving the apparent bestower of bounty, while forgetting the true Bestower of Bounty, is far worse. O soul! If you wish to avoid such stupidity, give and receive in God's name. Begin and act, to the very end, in His name. This will suffice you.

The Fourteenth Gleam's second station

I expound upon six of the innumerable mysteries of the *basmala*: In the Name of God, the Merciful, the Compassionate.[4] Even though addressed particularly to myself, I call it the "Second station of the Fourteenth Gleam." May it benefit those with whom I am associated spiritually and whose souls are wiser than mine. The argument touches the heart rather than the mind, and seeks to content the spirit rather than to regard rational proofs.

In the Name of God,
the Merciful, the Compassionate.

---

[4] A bright light from the *basmala* concerning Divine Mercy touched my dimmed mind from afar. I wanted to record it as notes and then pursue and gather its light in 20 to 23 sections of "Mysteries." Alas, I have not been able to do this yet, and my 20 to 30 have been brought down to 6.

> [The Queen] said: "Chieftains, here delivered to me is a letter worthy of respect. It is from Solomon, and is: In the Name of God, the Merciful, the Compassionate." (27:29-30)

FIRST MYSTERY: Three stamps of Lordship are impressed upon the face of the universe, Earth, and humanity. They are one within the other, and each carries a pattern of the others:

DIVINITY: We see this in how all entities in the universe help and cooperate with each other, and in their general interconnectedness and reciprocity. The referent is In the Name of God.

DIVINE MERCIFULNESS: We see this in the mutuality of likeness and form, the orderliness and harmony, and the grace and compassion in disposing, raising, and administering plants and animals. The referent is the Merciful, in In the Name of God, the Merciful.

DIVINE COMPASSION: We see this in the subtleties of Divine Goodness, the delicate adjustments of Divine Mildness, and the scattering of the light of Divine Compassion on the face of our own comprehensive nature. The referent is the *Compassionate*, in *In the Name of God, the Merciful, the Compassionate*.

Thus the *basmala* is the holy expression of Divine Oneness' three stamps. They form a luminous line on the page of the universe, a robust stay, and a golden thread. Revealed from above us, the tip of *basmala* rests upon humanity, a miniature of the universe and its fruit. The *basmala* links the world to the Divine Throne and is a stairway for our ascent thereto.

SECOND MYSTERY: Divine Unity is evident in the boundless multiplicity of individualized creatures. So as not to overwhelm our minds all at once, the Qur'an, being a miracle of exposition, constantly reiterates the manifestation of Oneness[5] within Unity—the manifestation of a Divine Name on all beings.

Consider this analogy: The sun encompasses innumerable things in its light. But to hold the totality of its light in our minds, we would need a vast conceptual and perceptual power. So lest the sun be forgotten, all shining objects reflect its properties (light and heat) as best they can and so manifest its being the sun. This manifestation is reciprocated, for those properties (heat, light, and

---
[5] Oneness: The concentration of the Divine Names' manifestations on one thing.

the color spectrum) encompass the objects that the sun is facing.

Just as God's Oneness, His being Eternally Besought, and His Divine Names are manifested in everything, particularly in sentient creatures and especially in our mirror-like nature, each Divine Name related to creatures encompasses all creatures through Divine Unity. Thus the Qur'an constantly draws our attention to the stamp of Divine Oneness within Divine Unity, lest our minds be overwhelmed by Unity and our hearts become heedless of the Pure and Holy Essence. The *basmala* indicates the three important aspects of the stamp of Divine Unity.

THIRD MYSTERY: Divine Mercy causes the universe to rejoice. It gives the spark of light and life to dark entities, and nurtures and raises up creatures struggling with their endless need. It causes the universe to be directed toward humanity, just as a tree is directed toward its fruit, and to hasten to our assistance. It fills and lights up boundless space, an otherwise void and empty world, making it rejoice. For transient humanity, Divine Mercy also appoints eternity and the rank of the creature addressed and beloved of the One, Eternal before and after eternity.

Since Divine Mercy is so powerful a truth, so inviting, mild, helpful, and worthy of love, say: *In the Name of God, the Merciful, the Compassionate.* Cling to this truth, and be rescued from endless desolation and need. Draw near to the Sovereign, Eternal before and after eternity, and become the one He addresses, befriends, and loves.

Why do all entities gather around humanity with purpose and foresight, and hasten to meet our needs with perfect orderliness and grace? Do they recognize us and so run to help us—as irrational as it is, in many respects, impossible? Or do we, who have no power, have the power of the mightiest, absolute sovereign? Or does this help reach us via the recognition of One Absolutely Powerful behind the veil of the visible universe? In other words, all entities recognize us because the One, All-Knowing and Compassionate, is acquainted with and recognizes us.

Consider this: How could the All-Majestic One, Who causes all entities to turn toward you with their hands outstretched to help you, not know, see, or be aware of you when you are in need? He teaches you that He knows you through His Mercy. So know Him, and reverently show that you do. Understand with conviction that Divine Mercy's truth subjects the universe to your service, even though you are a slight, transient, wholly feeble, powerless, and needy creature.[6]

Such Mercy requires total and sincere gratitude as well as honest and ardent reverence. Say: *In the Name of God, the Merciful, the Compassionate,* which expresses and interprets such feelings. Make it the means of admission to His Mercy, an intercessor and advocate at the Court of the All-Merciful.

Divine Mercy's presence and actuality is as clear as the sun. A center-patterned tapestry is woven by positioning and sequencing the warp and weft and then gathered to the center. In the same way, bright threads extending from manifesting Divine Names weaves a seal of such compassion, a tapestry of such gentle mildness, a pattern of such goodness within the stamp of

---

[6] Divine Mercy also includes (Divine) Wisdom, Grace, Knowledge, and Power.

Mercy, that it is impressed upon the mind more brilliantly than the sun.

The Gracious All-Merciful One, Who causes everything to serve life; Who demonstrates His Compassion in the self-sacrifice, the extraordinary sweetness of compassion, of motherhood in plants and animals; Who subjects animate life to humanity and thereby displays our importance and status as the finest and loveliest weave from the Divine Lordship as well as His Mercy's brilliance—that One has, due to His lack of need, made His Mercy the acceptable intercessor for His sentient creatures and humanity.

If you are truly human, say: "O humanity: *In the Name of God, the Merciful, the Compassionate.*" Seek and find that intercessor. Nothing but Divine Mercy brings to life, nurtures, and administers all plant and animal species. It neither overlooks nor confuses one with another, but raises each at the right time and with perfect order, wisdom, and goodness. It then impresses the Seal of Divine Oneness upon Earth's surface. Just as Divine Mercy's existence is as certain as the existence of Earth's creatures, each creature also is a proof.

The Seal of Mercy and Divine Oneness is impressed upon Earth and upon humanity's nature. The Mercy stamped upon us is not less than the Compassion and Mercy stamped upon the universe. Our nature is comprehensive, as we are the weave's center and the Divine Names' focal point.

How could the One Who gives you this face, Who impresses upon it Mercy's stamp and Oneness' seal, leave you to your own devices? How could He consider you of no account, have no regard for your actions, and so make all creation, which is directed toward you, futile and wasteful? How could He make the Tree of Creation worthless and rotten with decayed fruit? Would He cause His Mercy to be denied when it is as obvious as the sun, and His Wisdom, which is as clear as light? Neither can be doubted or considered to contain any defect.

You can ascend to the throne of Divine Mercy by *In the Name of God, the Merciful, the Compassionate.* Grasp its importance by looking at the beginning of each Qur'anic *sura* (chapter), all worthwhile books and good actions. A clear argument for this phrase's greatness, a greatness determined by Him, is the comment of Imam Shafi'i[7]: "Although the *basmala* is a single verse, it was revealed 114 times in the Qur'an."

FOURTH MYSTERY: Divine Unity is manifested within the boundless multiplicity [of individualized creatures]. To say: *You alone do we worship* (1:5) is not enough, for our minds wander [from Reality]. Our heart would have to be as comprehensive as Earth to observe the One in His Oneness behind the Unity within the totality of individualized entities, and then say: *You alone do We worship, and from You alone do We seek help* (1:5). Thus, the seal of Divine Oneness must be apparent on all entities' minds and species, just as on each individualized entity.

In addition, they should remember the One in His Oneness. This need is met by the Divine

---

[7] Al-Shafi'i (d. 820): Muslim legal scholar, founder of the Shafi'i legal school. He developed a new synthesis of Islamic legal thought. Most of the ideas were already familiar, but he structured them in a new way. He mainly dealt with what the sources of Islamic law were and how they could be applied by the law to contemporary events. His *Al-Risala*, written during the last 5 years of his life, entitles him to be called the "father of Muslim jurisprudence." (Ed.)

Oneness being shown within the stamp of Divine Mercy. As a result, everyone at every level can turn to the Pure and Holy One and, by saying: *You alone do we worship, and from You alone do we seek help* (1:5), address Him directly.

To express this mighty mystery and point to the seal of Divine Mercy, the All-Wise Qur'an abruptly juxtaposes individualized detail with totality, small with large, particular with general. To prevent the mind from wandering and the heart from drowning, to allow the spirit to find its True Object of Worship directly, it broaches such subjects as our creation and speaking, the fine details of the favors and wisdom in our features, while mentioning the creation of the heavens and Earth. This truth is miraculously shown in *And among His signs is the creation of the heavens and Earth, and the varieties in your languages and in your colors* (30:22).

The stamp of Divine Unity, being within innumerable creatures and limitless multiplicity, is of various kinds and degrees. They are as in concentric circles, from the greatest to the smallest. But however clear that Unity is, it is still a Unity within multiplicity and cannot be truly addressed by observers. Thus the stamp of Divine Oneness must be behind the Unity, so that individuality does not call to mind multiplicity, and so that a way may be opened up to the heart directly before the Pure and Holy One.

Also, a most entrancing design, radiant light, agreeable sweetness, pleasing beauty, and powerful truth have been placed upon the stamp of Divine Oneness to draw our attention and hearts to it. Mercy's vigor draws sentient beings' attention and attracts them to it. It enables them to attain to the seal of Oneness, to serve the One in His Oneness, and thereby manifest the true address of: *You alone do we worship, and from You alone do We seek help* (1:5).

Thus *In the Name of God, the Merciful, the Compassionate*, the index of the Chapter of Opening (*Surat al-Fatiha*) and an epitome of the Qur'an, is the sign and interpreter of this mighty mystery. Whoever attains to it may ascend through the levels of Divine Mercy; whoever causes it to speak may learn the mysteries of Divine Mercy and see the lights of Divine Compassion and Pity.

FIFTH MYSTERY: There is a Tradition[8] to the effect that God created humanity in the form of the All-Merciful One. Its extravagant interpretation by some Sufis does not accord with the fundamentals of belief.[9] Some ecstatic Sufis claim that our spiritual nature is "in the form of the All-Merciful." Immersed in their confusing contemplative trances, they might be excused for expressing mistaken views. If others consider such views acceptable, they also are in error.

---

[8] The Arabic word *hadith*, commonly translated into English as Tradition, literally means "news, story, communication, or conversation," whether religious or secular, historical or recent. In the Qur'an, this words appears in religious (39:23, 68:44), secular or general (6:68), historical (20:9), and current or conversational (66:3) contexts. The Prophet used it in a similar sense, for example, when he said: "The best *hadith* is the Qur'an" (Bukhari). However, the *Muhaddithin* (Traditionists [scholars of Traditions]) state that the word stands for "what was transmitted on the Prophet's authority, his deeds, sayings, tacit approvals, or descriptions of his physical appearance." Jurists do not include this last item in their definition. (Tr.)

[9] Sufism: A spiritual Islamic belief and practice in which Muslims seek to find divine love and knowledge through the ways particular to it. Its adherents are known, in the West, as Sufis. (Ed.)

The Pure and Holy God, Who orders and administers the universe as easily as if it were a palace or a house, Who turns galaxies as if they were particles and sends them travelling through space with wisdom and grace, Who dispatches the minutest particles as if they were obedient officials, has no equal or match, no partner or opposite. According to: *There is nothing like to Him, and He is the All-Hearing, the All-Seeing* (42:11), He has no form, likeness, or peer. Nothing resembles or is similar to Him. On the other hand, according to: *And His is the highest similitude in the Heavens and Earth, and He is Exalted in Might, the All-Wise* (30:27), humanity can conceive of His acts, Attributes, and Names via allegory and comparison. Thus the Tradition's intended meaning is: "Humanity's form, in its totality, reflects the Divine Name the All-Merciful."

This Divine Name is evident via the light of all Names manifested in the universe, and on Earth through innumerable evidences of God's absolute Lordship. In the same way, the All-Merciful is fully manifested, in miniature, in our comprehensive form.

A further indication may be derived from the following analogy: Animate creation and humanity are loci of evidences of the Necessarily Existent One, proofs and mirrors to the All-Merciful, All-Compassionate. These proofs are so certain, clear, and evident that just as we might say that a mirror reflecting the sun "has the form of (or is like) the sun" (emphasizing the brilliant evidence of the sun's light), we also might say: "Humanity has the All-Merciful One's form," stressing the clear evidence within us, and the completeness of the connection in Him, of the All-Merciful. Therefore, the more moderate and balanced believers in the Unity of Being said: "There is no existent but He," expressing the evidence's clarity and the connection's perfection.

> O God, O All-Merciful, All-Compassionate. Through the truth of *In the Name of God, the Merciful, the Compassionate,* have mercy on us according to Your being the Compassionate. Open to our understanding the mysteries of this phrase, according to Your being the Merciful. Amen.

SIXTH MYSTERY: O unhappy humanity laboring under limitless impotence and unending need. Understand Divine Mercy's value as a means and an intercessor. It is the means to a Glorious Sovereign in Whose army vast galaxies and minute particles serve together in perfect obedience and harmony. That Glorious Sovereign, the One, Eternal before and after eternity, is the Eternally Besought—everything needs Him Who has no need.

He is infinitely rich and does not need the universe or its entities. Everything is under His authority and direction, obedient before His Majesty and Greatness, awed and prostrate before His Sublimity. This is the Divine Mercy, and it is for you. It uplifts you to the Presence of One without need, the Eternal Sovereign Who befriends you and addresses you as His well-loved servant.

Yet just as you cannot draw close to the sun, even though its light is reflected and manifested to you through your mirror, you are infinitely far from the Light of the Pure and Holy One, the Eternal before and after eternity. You cannot draw closer to Him unless the Light of His Mercy makes Him closer to you.

Whoever finds this Mercy finds an eternal treasure of unfailing light. This Mercy can be reached through the Sunna[10] of the most noble Prophet, its most brilliant exemplar and representative, its most eloquent voice and herald, who the Qur'an hails as "a mercy for all the worlds." He can be reached by calling the blessings of God upon him, for the intent of this prayer is mercy. As a prayer of mercy for the living embodiment of Divine Mercy, it reaches the "mercy to all the worlds."

So use this prayer to reach him, and make him the way through which you can reach the Mercy of the Most Merciful of the Merciful. All Muslims say this prayer for the "mercy to all the worlds," which is synonymous with Mercy. Doing so is a dazzling demonstration of how precious a gift Divine Mercy is, and how broad is its sphere.

In conclusion, the most precious jewel in Mercy's treasury is its door-keeper: Prophet

---

[10] The Sunna is the record of the Messenger's every act, word, and confirmation, as well as the second source of Islamic legislation and life (the Qur'an is the first one). In addition to establishing new principles and rules, the Sunna clarifies the ambiguities in the Qur'an by expanding upon what is mentioned only briefly in it, specifies what is unconditional, and enables generalizations from what is specifically stated and particularizations from what is generally stated. (Ed.)

Muhammad. The first key is *In the Name of God, the Merciful, the Compassionate,* and the easiest key to use is praying for the Prophet.

> O God! For the sake of the mysteries of *In the Name of God, the Merciful, the Compassionate,* bestow blessings and peace on the one You sent as a mercy to all the worlds in accordance with Your Mercy and the honor due to him, and on his Family and Companions. Grant us mercy so that we are free of need for the mercy of any, among your creatures, other than You. Amen. Glory be to You! We have no knowledge save what You have taught us. Truly, you are the All-Knowing, the All-Wise.

The Second Word

The Way to Contentment

If you wish to understand how to enjoy great contentment and blessing through belief, and how to experience fulfillment and ease, listen to the following parable:

Two people travel for both pleasure and business. The first one is conceited and pessimistic, and so ends up in what he considers a most wicked country. He sees himself surrounded by poor and hopeless people tormented by bullies and living ruined lives, for everyone suffers the same misery. Trying to forget everything by intoxicants transforms everyone into a stranger or an enemy. He has awful visions of corpses and orphans, and his soul is plunged into torment.

The second person, a God-serving, decent, and fair-minded man, goes to a country that he considers quite excellent. Seeing a universal festival, he finds joy and happiness in every corner, and a house for remembering God overflowing with rapture. He sees the celebrations of a general discharge from duties (death) accompanied by cries of good wishes and thanks.

Hearing a drum and a band for enlisting soldiers with happy calls of "God is the Greatest" and "There is no god but God," he becomes happy at his own joy and that of others. He enjoys a comfortable trade and thanks God.

When he meets his relative, he understands the latter's situation and says: "You've become crazy. The bad and ugly things you see come from and reflect your inner world. You imagine laughter to be weeping, and discharge from duties to be sack and pillage. Come to your senses and clean your heart, so that this inauspicious veil will be raised from your eyes and you may see the truth. This is an orderly, prosperous, and civilized country with a powerful, compassionate, and just ruler. Things are not as you see or think." The man comes to his senses and is full of regret: "Yes, I've really gone crazy because of all those intoxicants. Thank you. May God be pleased with you for rescuing me from such a hellish state."

O my soul! The first person represents an unbeliever or a heedless sinner who sees this world as a place of general mourning, all living things as weeping orphans due to the pain of separation and decay, people and animals as lonely and uncivilized creatures cut down by death, and great masses (mountains and oceans) as terrible corpses without souls. His unbelief and misguidance breed great anxieties that torture him.

The second person believes in and affirms God Almighty. He sees the world as a place where people praise Him, a practice arena for people and animals, and an examination hall for people and jinn. Animals and humanity are demobilized so that after death believers can travel in spiritual enjoyment to the other world—for this world needs a new generation to populate and work in it.

All animals and people enter this world for a reason. All living things are as soldiers or officials, happy with their appointed task. The sound we hear is their praise and glorifying as they begin, or their pleasure while working, or their thanksgiving as they finish. Believers see all things as obedient servants, friendly officials, a lovable book of their Most Generous Master and All-Compassionate Owner.

Many more such beautiful, sublime, and pleasurable truths arise from belief. This is because belief bears the seed of what is, in effect, a Tuba tree of Paradise, whereas unbelief contains the seed of a Zaqqum tree of Hell. Safety and well-being are found only in Islam and belief. Therefore, always thank God, saying: "Praise be to God for Islam and perfect belief."

THE THIRD WORD

Choosing the Right Way

In the Name of God,
the Merciful, the Compassionate.

O you people, worship... (2:21)

If you want to understand the bliss and benefit that come with prayer, and the loss and destruction that come with vice, dissipation, and ignoring God's commands, listen to this short parable:

Two soldiers are told to go to a far town. Travelling together, they come to a fork and meet a wise person who says: "The right road is risk-free, and nine out of ten travelers meet with great advantage but no difficulty. The left road offers no benefit, and nine out of ten travelers suffer great loss. Both roads are the same length. But there is one difference: Those who take the left road, which has no rules or someone in charge, travel without equipment or arms, and so appear comfortable and at ease. Those who take the right road must submit to military rules, carry their own food, and a heavy weapon in case of attack."

One soldier takes the right fork. Shouldering his heavy load, his heart and soul are simultaneously freed of any burdensome debt and fear. Travelling in peace, the townspeople he meets treat him as an honest soldier who fully performs his duties. The other soldier takes the left fork. Carrying nothing heavy, his heart and soul nevertheless suffer from countless dangers and anxieties. He is constantly fearful and in need. When he reaches any town, he is treated as a rebel and fugitive.

Now, my undisciplined and carnal soul, pay attention. The first soldier represents an obedient servant of God; the second soldier represents rebels and those who follow their own desire. The road is the lifeline coming from the world of souls, passing through this world and the grave, and continuing toward the Hereafter.

The heavy load and weapon are worship and piety. Prayer seems to be a strenuous demand, but in reality gives indescribable peace and comfort. Those who pray recite *ashhadu an la ilaha illa Allah* (I bear witness that there is no god but

God),[11] the Creator and All-Provider. Only He can give harm and benefit. He is the All-Wise Who does nothing useless, the All-Compassionate Whose mercy and bounty are abundant. The believing soldier sees in every event a door to the wealth of God's Mercy and knocks on it via supplication. Realizing that his Lord and Sustainer controls everything, he takes refuge in Him. Putting his trust in and fully submitting to God, he resists evil. His belief gives him total confidence.

As with every good action, courage arises from belief in and loyal devotion to God. As with every bad action, cowardice arises from misguidance. If Earth were to explode, those servants of God with truly illuminated hearts would not be afraid—they might even consider it a marvel of the Eternally Besought's Power. A rationalist but unbelieving philosopher might tremble at the sight of a comet, lest it should strike Earth (as did some Americans to the recent sighting of Haley's comet).

Our ability to meet our endless demands is negligible. We are threatened with afflictions that our

---

[11] The Islamic profession of faith. Anyone who says it is considered a Muslim, and is entitled to all the rights and benefits, as well as regulations and duties, of Islam. (Ed.)

own strength cannot withstand. Our strength is limited to what we can reach, yet our wishes and demands, suffering and sorrow, are as wide as our imagination.

Anyone not wholly blind to the truth knows that our best option is to submit to God, to worship, believe, and have confidence in Him. A safe road is preferable to a dangerous one, even one with a tiny probability of safe passage. The way of belief leads one safely to endless bliss with near certainty; the way of unbelief and transgression is not profitable and has a near certainty of endless loss.[12] Even its travelers agree on this truth, as do countless experts and people of insight and observation.

Thus, just like the other world's bliss, happiness here depends upon submitting to God and being His devoted servant. So always praise Him, saying: "Praise be to God for obedience and success in His way," and thank Him that we are Muslims.

---

[12] The author uses *near certainty*, as opposed to *absolute certainty*, out of respect for His absolutely free will. God cannot be made or regarded as obliged to put believers in Paradise and unbelievers in Hell, for He does whatever He wills. But as He promised that He would reward those who believe and do good deeds with eternal bliss in Paradise, and punish those who do not believe in Hell, He will fulfill His promise. (Tr.)

THE FOURTH WORD

The Prescribed Prayers' Value

In the Name of God,
the Merciful, the Compassionate.

The prescribed prayers (*salat*) are Islam's pillars. To fully understand their importance, consider this parable: A ruler gives each of his two servants 24 gold coins and sends them to a beautiful farm that is 2 months' travel away. He tells them: "Use this money to buy your ticket, your supplies, and what you will need after you arrive. After traveling for a day, you will reach a transit station. Chose a method of transportation that you can afford."

The servants leave. One spends only a little money before reaching the station, and so wisely that his master increases it a thousandfold. The other servant gambles away 23 of the 24 coins before reaching the station. The first servant advises the second one: "Use this coin to buy your ticket, or else you'll have to walk and suffer hunger. Our master is generous. Maybe he'll forgive you. Maybe you can take a plane, so we can reach the farm in a day. If not, you'll have to go on foot and endure 2 months of hunger while crossing the desert." If he ignores his friend's advice, anyone can see what will happen.

Now listen to the explanation, those of you who do not pray, as well as you, my soul that is not inclined toward prayer. The ruler is our Creator. One servant represents religious people who pray with fervor; the other represents people who do not like to pray. The 24 coins are the 24 hours of a day. The farm is heaven, the transit station is the grave, and the journey is from the grave to eternal life. People cover that journey at different times according to their deeds and conduct. Some of the truly devout pass in a day 1,000 years like lightning, while others pass 50,000 years with the speed of imagination. The Qur'an alludes to this truth in 22:47 and 70:4.[13]

---

[13] ... *A day in the sight of your Lord is like 1,000 years of your reckoning, and ... The angels and the spirit ascend to Him in a day, the measure of which is 50,000 years of your reckoning, respectively.*

The ticket is the prescribed prayers, which can be prayed in an hour. If you spend 23 hours in worldly affairs and do not reserve the remaining hour for the prescribed prayers, you are a foolish loser. You may be tempted to use half of your money for a lottery being played by 1,000 people. Your chance of winning is 1:1,000, while those who pray have a 99 percent chance of winning. If you do not use at least one coin to gain an inexhaustible treasure, something is wrong with you.

Prayer comforts the soul and the mind and is easy for the body. Furthermore, correct intention transforms our deeds and conduct into worship. Thus our short lifetime is spent for the sake of eternal life in the other world, and our transient life gains a kind of permanence.

THE FIFTH WORD

The Right Training for Believers

> In the Name of God
> the Merciful, the Compassionate.
>
> Surely God is with those Who refrain
> from disobeying Him in awe of Him and
> who do good deeds (as if they saw Him).
> (16:128)

The allegory below shows how necessary it is to pray and avoid major sins, and that both tasks are directly related to our own nature:

During a war, one private is well-trained and conscientious while another is a recruit and a slave to his self. The first one attends training exercises and struggles against the enemy. He never worries about rations and allowances, because he knows the government will supply the necessary military equipment, food, and medical care. All he has to do is train for war and fight for the country. He helps out by supplying food and working in the kitchen. When asked what he is doing, he responds: "Some of the state's chores." He does not say he is working for his living. But the other soldier does not train or fight, for: "It's none of my business. It's a government matter." He cares only about his livelihood, and so deserts the battlefront and goes to the marketplace.

The first soldier advises him: "Brother, you're supposed to be training to fight for the country. That's why you're here. The king will meet your needs, because that's his duty. You can't meet all your needs regardless of time or place. As we're in a state of war, you might be accused of desertion or rebellion and be punished. We have our duty, and the king has his. We prepare to fight, and the king meets our needs." Imagine what trouble the second soldier will be in if he ignores his friend's words.

O my indolent soul! The battlefield represents the tumult of worldly life. The army divided into regiments represents humanity divided into nations. That particular battalion stands for an Islamic society. One soldier is a devout and pious Muslim who knows what he is asked to do and so struggles against his self and Satan. The other soldier is a sinner who ignores his duties as a servant, commits many sins, and is so obsessed with his rations and allowances that he even accuses the true Sustainer.

Training represents the daily prayers and other duties required of believers. The war stands for the process through which the spirit achieves everlasting salvation—fighting carnal passions. These two duties are easily understood: The first (the creation and maintenance of life) is the Creator's responsibility, while the second (beseeching from the Creator and Sustainer and relying on Him totally) is ours.

Only He Who gives life, a most brilliant miracle of the Eternally Besought's art and a wonder of the Master's Wisdom, sustains life with provision. Do you need convincing? The weakest and simplest animals are the best fed. The least capable and most vulnerable creatures, such as babies or new-born animals, get the best food. Obtaining food has nothing to do with strength or free will, but of being in need and suffering shortages. See how trees and animals, fish and foxes, as well as babies and young animals and adults and beasts are fed. This should convince you.

Those who ignore their daily prayers to pursue their livelihood are like the soldier who neglects his exercises, deserts the front for fear of hunger, and wanders around the marketplace. In contrast, seeking one's rations from Earth—the kitchen of the All-Generous Provider's Mercy—after praying and not burdening others is fine and proper. This too is a kind of worship.

Furthermore, our nature and spiritual being show that we are created to worship God. As for our physical powers and ability to live here, we are in worse shape than sparrows. But in respect to our knowledge, understanding our need, and supplication and worship, which are necessary for our spiritual life and the life of the Hereafter, we are the king and commander of all animate creatures.

O my soul. If you consider this world your major goal and work for it, you will remain only a soldier with no more control over your affairs than a sparrow. But if you move toward the Hereafter, consider this world a field to be sown, a preparation for the other world, and act accordingly, you become the ruler of the animal kingdom, a supplicant of Almighty God, and His favored or indulged guest in this world. You can choose either option. So ask for guidance and success in His way from the Most Compassionate of the Compassionate.

THE SIXTH WORD

The Supreme Transaction

In the Name of God,
the Merciful, the Compassionate.

> Verily God bought from the believers their selves and their possessions in exchange for Paradise. (9:111)

If you want to understand how profitable and honorable such a transaction is, listen to the following parable: A king entrusted two servants with one estate each, including all necessary workshops, machinery, horses, weapons, and other equipment. But as it was wartime, when everything is in flux, this merciful and compassionate king sent his noblest officer to them with the following message:

> Sell me the entrusted property so that I may keep it for you. Don't let it be destroyed in vain. After the war is over, I'll return it to you in better shape than it was before. It's your property in trust, and I'll pay a higher price for it. The machin-

ery and tools will be used in my name at my workbench. Both the price and the fee for their use shall be increased, maybe a thousandfold. I'll give all the profit to you. You are weak and poor, and can't pay for these great tasks. Let me take care of the expenses and equipment, and give you the income and profit. You can use it until demobilization. Consider the five advantages of this transaction.

If you don't sell the property to me, consider this. You can't preserve what you possess, and so will lose what you now hold. It will go in vain, and you will miss out on the high price I offer you. All the delicate, precious tools and fine scales that are ready to be used will lose their value, since there are no metals worthy of their use. You'll have to find some way to administer and preserve them. Moreover, you'll be punished for betraying your trust. So consider the ways you may lose.

If you sell your property to me, you'll become my soldier and act in my name. Far from being a mere recruit or irregular, you'll be an honored and free officer of an exalted monarch.[14]

---

[14] Some may see a threat here. However, human existence here is a reality out of human will. Therefore it is much more than a bargain, for God's creation of us is a pure blessing.

After the two men had listened to this gracious decree, one said: "I'm honored and happy to sell. Thank you so much." The other was as proud, arrogant, selfish, and dissipated as Pharaoh. As if he would stay on that estate forever, he ignored the earthquakes and tumults and said: "No! Who is this king? I won't sell my property or diminish my comfort." After a while, the first man reached such a high rank that everyone envied his position. He had the king's favor and lived happily in the king's palace. The other one fell so low that everyone pitied him but realized that he deserved his position. As a result of his mistake, he forfeited his happiness and property, and suffered punishment and torment.

How many people complain of being in the world? Is there anybody who does not love life? Only those misusing their willpower and engulfed in dissipation complain about life. No true believer complains. Whatever we do not like in life and in the world is due to the fact that we neglect our responsibilities as the most honored of beings. God's informing us of how to act in life and then rewarding us with eternal happiness is as great and infinite a blessing as eternity. If some still see a threat, that threat is also pure blessing, as it compels us to find the straight way and attain happiness in both worlds, where a promise is not enough for weak-willed, spiritually corrupt, obstinate persons to change their ways. (Tr.)

Now, O soul full of caprice, consider the truth shown here. The king is the Monarch, Eternal before and after eternity, your Lord and Creator. That which He has entrusted to you represent your body, spirit, and heart, and so on, as well as your outer and inner senses (e.g., sight, taste, intelligence, imagination). The officer is the Messenger; the compassionate decree is the Qur'an, which states: *God has bought from the believers their selves and their possessions in exchange for Paradise* (9:111). The surging battlefield is the tempestuous surface of a world in flux, and causes us to reflect.

People ask: "Everything will leave our hands, perish, and be lost. Maybe there is a way to make it eternal, to preserve it?" While engaged in such thoughts, they suddenly hear the Qur'an's heavenly voice say: "There is a beautiful and easy way that offers five advantages or profits." What is this way? To sell the trust to its real Owner. The resulting five profits are:

FIRST PROFIT: Transient property becomes everlasting. This waning life, when given to the Eternal and Self-Subsistent Being of Majesty and spent for His sake, is transmuted into permanence and gives everlasting fruits. The moments of one's present life vanish and rot, as do kernels and seeds. But then the flowers of happiness open and bloom in the Realm of Eternity, and each presents a luminous and reassuring aspect in the Intermediate Realm.

SECOND PROFIT: The price paid is Paradise.

THIRD PROFIT: The value of each bodily limb and sense is increased a thousandfold. For example, if you use your intelligence for the sake of the self, it becomes an ill-omened, destructive, and debilitating instrument burdening you with sad sorrows of the past and terrifying fears of the future. This is why sinful people frequently resort to drunkenness or other frivolous pleasures. But if you sell your intelligence to its true Owner and use it on His behalf, it becomes like a mysterious key unlocking Compassion's infinite treasure-house and wisdom-filled vaults, and elevates you to the rank of a pious and righteous guide deserving eternal happiness.

The eye is a window through which the spirit looks at this world. If you use it on behalf of the self, by gazing at transient, impermanent beauties and spectacles, it panders to lust and other carnal desires. But if you sell it to its All-Seeing Maker and use it on His behalf and within His limits, it rises to the rank of a reader of the Great Book of the Universe,[15] a witness of the miracles of His creation, a blessed bee sucking on the blossoms of Mercy in the garden of this world.

If you use your taste on behalf of the self and for the sake of your tongue or stomach, it sinks to the level of a gatekeeper at the stomach's stable, a watchman at its factory. But if you sell it to the Noble Provider, the sense of taste rises to the rank of a skilled overseer at Divine Compassion's treasure house, a grateful inspector in the kitchens of the Eternally Besought's Power.

O intelligence, be careful! Think of what is an instrument of destruction and what is a key to all being. O eye! See the difference between an abominable panderer and a learned overseer of

---

[15] In Said Nursi's thought, God created the universe as a "book" to be "read" by those who want to learn of and draw close to Him. The universe's order, regularity, interconnectedness, functioning, and so on display some of his Names and Attributes. Others are displayed through the animate and inanimate members of His creation, such as the All-Compassionate, All-Providing, All-Merciful, Forgiver, and so on. (Ed.)

the Divine Library! O tongue! Taste well the difference between a stable doorkeeper or a factory watchman and the trustee of the treasure house of God's Mercy!

When you compare all other instruments, faculties, and limbs to these, you understand that believers acquire a nature worthy of Paradise and unbelievers a nature conforming to Hell. Each attains its respective value. Due to their belief, believers use what the Creator has entrusted to them on His behalf and within His limits. Unbelievers betray the trust and use it for the sake of the carnal self.

FOURTH PROFIT: You are helpless and exposed to misfortune, indigence, uncountable needs, and impotence. Life's burden is very heavy. If you do not rely on the All-Powerful One of Majesty, trust in and submit to Him with full confidence, your conscience remains troubled by vain torment, pain and regret, all of which destroy your understanding. Eventually, you become beasts.

FIFTH PROFIT: Those who unveil the true nature of things and experience the truth agree that the reward for worshipping and glorifying God performed by your limbs, senses, and faculties will be given at the time of greatest need, in the form of Paradise's fruits.

If you refuse, you suffer the following fivefold loss:

FIRST LOSS: Your beloved property and offspring, your adored self and its caprice, your foolishly loved youth and life all are replaced by pain and sin.

SECOND LOSS: You are punished for betraying the trust, for you wrong yourself by using the most precious tools on the most worthless objects.

THIRD LOSS: By debasing your precious faculties to a level much inferior to animals, you insult and transgress God's Wisdom.

FOURTH LOSS: In your helplessness and poverty, you shoulder life's heavy burden and continually groan under the blows of transience and separation.

FIFTH LOSS: You convert the Compassionate One's fair gifts, meant to be used for laying the foundations of everlasting life and blessedness in the Hereafter, into ugliness. All they will be suitable for is opening the gates of Hell before you.

Why do many people not want to sell? Is it so hard? By no means! The resulting burdens are not hard. The limits of the permissible are broad and adequate for your desire, and so you do not need to indulge in what is forbidden. The duties imposed by God are light and few. To be His servant and soldier is an honor beyond description.

Your duty is to act and embark on all things in God's name, like a soldier, to receive and give on God's behalf, and to obey His permission and law. If you sin, seek His forgiveness by saying: "O Lord, forgive our sins and accept us as your servants. Entrust us with Your trust until the time of restitution arrives. Amen." And petition Him.

THE SEVENTH WORD

The Door to Human Happiness

Belief in the All-Mighty Creator and the Hereafter is precious, since such belief is used to reveal the universe and open the door to happiness. Patiently relying on the Creator, beseeching the Provider in gratitude, and seeking refuge in Him are invaluable medicines for all ailments. Heeding the Qur'an, abiding by its laws, praying, and refraining from major sins provide us with the documents and passport needed for our journey to Eternity.[16] They are a light for the grave and a provision for the next life.

---

[16] The major sins consist of associating partners with God; disrespecting one's parents; consuming the property of others, especially of orphans; engaging in usury; retreating when the army advances; slandering chaste women; committing crimes with a prescribed punishment (e.g., theft, fornication, adultery, murder); engaging in prohibited acts despite the Qur'an's or the Traditions' threat of a severe punishment for doing so in the next life; and deeds cursed by the Prophet. (Tr.)

If you want to understand this truth, understand the following story: Once a soldier in the middle of a battlefield found himself in frightening circumstances. He was wounded on his right and left sides. Behind him was a lion ready to tear him apart, and ahead of him his friends and comrades were being hanged. Beyond him lay the long road into exile.

A wise, pious person appeared on his right and said: "Don't despair. I'll give you two precious phrases that will render the lion harmless, like a horse, and make the gallows like a swing for your enjoyment. I'll give you two medicines that will heal your wounds and make them smell like roses. I'll also give you a ticket that allows you to travel the distance of years in one day. Try them and see if my words are true." The soldier did so. Finding his words true, the soldier believed and followed the person's advice.

Suddenly, a devilish man appeared on his left and said: "Let's enjoy ourselves, listen to music, and eat and drink these delicious things." He asked the soldier what he was mumbling. The soldier replied: "A sacred invocation,'" to which the man said: "Leave these complicated issues. Let's not ruin our comfort. What's that in your hands?" The soldier replied "Medicine." The man snorted: "Throw it away. There's nothing wrong with you. What's that paper with five seals upon it?" When the soldier said it was a ticket and a rations card, the man said: "Tear them up! How can you think of going anywhere on such a beautiful spring day?" This is how that devilish man tried to lead the soldier astray. The soldier eventually will be tempted to follow, for he is human and thus subject to deception.

To his right, the soldier suddenly hears a thunder-like voice: "Wake up! Don't be deceived. Say to that devil: 'If you can kill the lion, do so. If you can remove the gallows, do so. If you can heal my wounds, do so. If you can arrange it so that I don't need to leave this place, do so. Do these things, and then we can enjoy ourselves. If you cannot, be quiet!'"

To return to reality: The soldier represents each one of us. The lion is our appointed hour of death, while the gallows stand for our continual separation from friends. The two wounds are our infinite and troublesome impotence and our grievous and boundless poverty. The long journey goes from the World of Spirits to our life as an embryo, then to youth, old age, being laid out in the grave, life in the grave up to the Day of Resurrection, and passage over the Sirat bridge to begin eternal life in the Hereafter. The two talismans are belief in God and the Hereafter.

Understand: *Belief in the All-Mighty Creator and the Hereafter.* This precious talisman gives us peace of mind and God's Mercy. The lion, unable to act without His permission, becomes like an obedient horse. Thus the pious and learned, those who have a true understanding of death, are not afraid of dying and actually wish to die before their appointed time.

The passage of time, punctuated by separation from friends (because of death, represented by gallows), is transformed by belief in the Hereafter into a means to see the perpetually renewed and always colorful embroideries of God's wonderful acts, His Power's miracles, and His Compassion's manifestations. Its like is this: Since the "mirrors" reflecting the sunlight's colors are varied and replaced, the resulting views are even more beautiful.

The first medicine is patience and trusting in God, relying on His Power, and having confidence in His Wisdom. What is there to fear when, realizing our helplessness, we rely upon the Owner of *Be, and it is* (36:82)? Even when confronted with a most frightening situation and a great calamity, he says: *Verily, to God do we belong, and to Him is our return* (2:156), and places his trust in his Most Compassionate Lord with utmost serenity.

Thus the pious are content to realize their helplessness before God and put their hope in His decision. Surely there is pleasure in the fear of God. If a one-year old were asked what is the most pleasant thing he or she knows, the reply would be: "Being protected in my mother's warm embrace, conscious of my weakness and helplessness—instead of being punished as I expected." As a mother's compassion is only a small spark from God's Compassion, people of perfection take great pleasure in their helplessness and fear of God. Forsaking what is in their power, they take refuge in God and make their fear and helplessness a means of intercession before Him.

The other medicine is petitioning God with thanksgiving and contentment, and relying upon the Generous All-Provider's mercy. We ask and

God gives. How could the guests of a Generous All-Provider, Who has made Earth's surface as a table and the spring for flowers to put on that table, regard their own poverty and helplessness before God as unbearable? They could not. Their poverty and need become their appetite, and so they try to increase their poverty. This is why such people are proud of their poverty.[17]

The passport to Eternity comprises the five daily prayers, observing the other obligations, and avoiding the major sins. All people of discernment and learning agree that the only way to get a light, some provisions, and a vehicle for the long journey to Eternity is to abide by the Qur'an's laws and prohibitions. Science, philosophy, and craftsmanship alone are not worth much, for they only light the road as far as the grave.

The importance and ease of performing the five prayers and renouncing the seven major sins cannot be overemphasized. If you understand the truth here, you will turn to the one already astray and the one who wishes to lead you astray, and

---

[17] Poverty in the sense that God owns everything and we own nothing. It should not be confused with begging from people to meet one's worldly needs. (Ed.)

say: "If you can abolish death, impotence, and poverty, and close the door on the grave, do so. Otherwise, be still! In the greatest mosque of the universe, the Qur'an explains the universe, so let's listen to it. Let's become filled with its light and act according to its guidance. The Qur'an is the truth, since it comes from the Creator. It speaks the truth, spreading its light everywhere."

> O God, illuminate our hearts with the light of belief and the Qur'an. Enrich us with poverty in relation to You. Don't impoverish us with indifference toward You. We have given up our power and strength for Your sake and taken refuge in Your Power and strength, so make us among those who place their trust in You. Do not leave us to ourselves. Preserve us with Your preserving. Have mercy on us and all believers.

> Bestow blessings and peace upon our master Muhammad, Your servant and Prophet, Your chosen one and intimate friend—the beauty of Your Kingdom, the foremost of Your creation, the focus of Your affection, and the sun of Your guidance; the tongue of Your proofs, the embodiment of Your Compassion, the light of Your creation, and the noblest of Your creatures; the lamp of Your

Oneness among the multiplicity of Your creatures; the discloser of the mystery of Your creation; the herald of Your Lordship's Kingdom; the preacher of what pleases You; the proclaimer of Your Names' Treasures; the instructor of Your servants; the interpreter of Your signs; the mirror of Your Lordship's Beauty; the circle and compass of witnessing You and Your making us witnesses; Your beloved one and Messenger whom You sent as a mercy to the worlds—and upon his Family and Companions, his fellow Prophets and Messengers, Your angels brought near, and Your righteous servants. Amen.

THE EIGHTH WORD

The Necessity of Religion

In the Name of God,
the Merciful, the Compassionate.

God, there is no god but He, the Ever-Living, the Self-Subsistent. (2:255)

The religion with God is Islam. (3:19)

The following allegory explains the world and our spirit within it, and religion's nature and worth. It also explains how the absence of True Religion makes this world the darkest dungeon and the unbeliever the most unfortunate creature, and why belief in God's Existence and Unity, as well as reliance upon Him, opens the universe's secret sign and saves our souls from darkness.

Two brothers travel together. Coming to a fork in the road, they see a wise old man and ask him which way to take. He tells them that the right fork requires observance of the road's law and brings a certain security and happiness, while the left fork promises a certain kind of freedom as well as certain danger and distress. He tells them to choose. The well-disciplined brother, relying on God, takes the right fork and accepts dependence on law and order.

The other brother takes the left fork for the sake of freedom. He seems comfortable, but in fact feels no inner tranquillity. Reaching a desert, he suddenly hears the terrible sound of a beast that is about to attack him. He runs away and, seeing a waterless well 60 meters deep, jumps into it. Halfway down, he grabs a tree growing out of the wall to break his fall. The tree has two roots, both of which are being gnawed away by two rats, one white and the other black. Looking up, he sees the beast waiting for him. Looking down, he sees a horrible dragon almost at his feet, its large mouth open to receive him. Looking at the wall, he sees that it is covered with laboring insects. Looking again at the tree, he notices that although it is only a fig tree, it miraculously has many different fruits growing on it, such as walnuts and pomegranates.

Hanging in the well, he does not understand what has happened. He cannot imagine that somebody has caused all of these things to happen, for he cannot reason. Although inwardly distressed, and despite his spirit's and heart's complaints, his evil-commanding self pretends everything is fine and so ignores their weeping. Pretending that he is enjoying herself in a garden, he starts eating all kinds of fruits—for free. But some of them are poisonous and will harm him.

In a *hadith qudsi*, God says: "I will treat My servants in the way they think of Me."[18] This man sees everything happening to him as unimportant, and thus that is the way it is for him. He neither dies nor lives well, but merely persists in an agony of suspense.

The wiser and well-disciplined brother always thinks of the good, affirms the law, and feels secure and free. Finding beautiful flowers and fruits or ruined and ugly things in a garden, he focuses on what is good and beautiful. His brother cannot, for he has concerned himself with evil and finds no ease in such a garden. The wise brother lives according to: "Look on the good side of everything," and so is generally happy with everything.

---

[18] *Hadith Qudsi*: This is a specific category of sayings from the Prophet. The wording is the Prophet's, but the meaning belongs to God.

Upon reaching a desert and meeting a beast, he is afraid. But thinking that it must be serving someone, he is not so afraid. He also jumps down a well and, halfway down, catches hold of some tree branches. Noticing two rats gnawing at the tree's two roots, as well as the dragon below and the beast above, he finds himself in a strange situation.

But unlike his brother, he infers that everything has been arranged by someone and constitutes a sign. Thinking that he is being watched and examined, he understands that he is being directed and guided as a test and for a purpose. His curiosity aroused, he asks: "Who wants to make me know him?" Meanwhile, he remains patient and self-disciplined. This curiosity arouses in him a love for the sign's owner, which makes him want to understand the sign, what the events mean, and to acquire good qualities to please its owner.

He realizes that the tree is a fig tree, although it bears many kinds of fruit. He is no longer afraid, for he realizes that it is a sample catalogue of the unseen owner's fruits prepared for guests. Otherwise, one tree would not bear so many different fruits. He starts to pray earnestly and, as a result, the key to the secret is inspired in him. He declares: "O owner of this scene and events, I am in your hands. I take refuge in you and am at your service. I desire your approval and knowledge of you." The wall opens, revealing a door (the dragon's mouth) leading onto a wonderful, pleasant garden. Both the dragon and the beast become two servants inviting him in. The beast changes into a horse on which he rides.

And so, my lazy soul and imaginary friend! Let's compare their positions and see how good brings good and evil brings evil. The brother who took the left road of self-trust and self-willed freedom is about to fall into the dragon's mouth. He is always anxious and lonely, and considers himself a prisoner facing the attacks of wild beasts. He adds to his distress by eating apparently delicious but actually poisonous fruits that are only samples; they are not meant to be eaten for their own sake, but to persuade people to seek the originals and become customers of them. He changes his day into darkness. He wrongs herself, changing his situation into a hell-like one, so that he neither deserves pity nor has the right to complain.

In contrast, the brother who took the right way is in a fruitful garden and surrounded by servants.

He studies every different and beautiful incident in awe, and sees himself as an honored guest enjoying his generous host's strange and beautiful servants. He does not eat up the fig tree's fruits; rather, he samples them and, understanding reality, postpones his pleasure and enjoys the anticipation.

The first brother is like one who denies his favored situation in a summer garden surrounded by friends, and instead, becoming drunk, imagines himself among wild beasts in winter and complains thereof. Wronging himself and insulting his friends, he deserves no mercy. The other brother, who accepts trustingly what is given and observes the law, sees and accepts reality, which for him is beautiful. Respecting the owner of reality, he deserves mercy. Thus can we attain a partial understanding of: *Whatever good befalls you is from God, and whatever ill befalls you is from yourself* (4:79).

Reflecting upon the brothers, we see that one's inner self prepared a hell-like situation for him, corresponding to his own attitude of reality, whereas the other's potential goodness, positive intention, and good nature led him to a very favored and happy situation. Now, I say to my own inner self as well as to the reader's: If you desire success, follow the guidance of the Qur'an.

The gist of the allegory is as follows: One brother is a believer; the other is an unbeliever. The right road is that of the Qur'an and belief; the left road is that of unbelief and rebellion. The garden is human society and civilization, which contain both good and evil, cleanliness and pollution. A sensible person "takes what is clear and pleasant, leaves what is turbid and distressing," and proceeds with a tranquil heart. The desert is Earth, the beast is death, the well is our life, and 60 meters is our average lifespan of 60 years.

The tree in the well is life, the two rats gnawing on its roots are day and night, and the dragon is the grave's opening. For a believer, it is no more than a door opening onto the Garden. The insects are the troubles we face, and in reality are God's gentle warnings that prevent believers from becoming heedless. The fruits are the bounties of this world presented as samples from the blessings of the Hereafter, inviting customers toward the fruits of Paradise.[19] The sign shows the

---

[19] The tree with various fruits shows the seal of Divinity, Whose unique virtue is "to create everything out of one

secret will of God in creating. It is opened with belief, and its key is: "O God, there is no god but God; God, there is no god but He, the Ever-Living, the Self-Subsistent."

For one brother, the dragon's mouth (the grave) changes into a door to the Garden (Paradise). For the other, as for all unbelievers, the grave is the door to a place of trouble (Hell). The beast changes into an obedient servant, a disciplined and trained horse. In other words, for unbelievers death is a painful detachment from loved ones, an imprisonment after leaving the Paradise-like Earth. For believers, it is a means of reunion with dead friends and companions. It is like going to their eternal home of happiness, a formal invitation to pass into the eternal gardens, an occasion to receive the wage bestowed by the Most Compassionate and Merciful One's generosity for services rendered to Him, and a kind of retirement from the burden of life.

---

thing" and "to change everything into one thing"; to make various plants and fruits from the same soil; to create all living things from one drop of water; and to nourish and sustain all living things in the same manner but through different foods. (Tr.)

In sum, those who pursue this transient life place themselves in Hell, even though they stay in what appears —to them—as a paradise on Earth. Those who seek the eternal life find peace and happiness in both worlds. Despite all troubles, they thank God and patiently conclude that all of this is merely a waiting room opening onto Heaven.

> O God, make us among the people of happiness, salvation, the Qur'an, and belief! Amen. O God, bestow peace and blessings upon our master Muhammad, and upon his Family and Companions, to the number of all letters contained in the Qur'an, reflected by the permission of the Most Compassionate One in the sound waves of each word recited by Qur'anic reciters from its first revelation to the end of time. Have mercy on us and our parents, and upon all believers to the number of those words, through Your Mercy, O Most Merciful of the Merciful. Amen. All praise be to God, Lord of all the worlds.

THE NINTH WORD

The Different Prayer Times

In the Name of God,
the Merciful, the Compassionate.

> Glory be to God whenever you reach evening and whenever you rise in the morning. All praise is for Him in the Heavens and on Earth, in the late afternoon, and whenever you reach the noon. (30:17-18)

You ask me, fellow Muslims, why the five daily prayers must be prayed at specific times. I will give just one of the many reasons for this. Each prayer time is the opening of a significant turning point, a mirror to the Divine disposal of power as well as the universal Divine bounties therein. We are told to pray at those specific times to give more adoration and glory to the All-Powerful One of Majesty, and to give more thanks for the bounties accumulated between any two periods. To comprehend this subtle and profound meaning a little better, consider these five points:

FIRST POINT: Each prayer stands for praising, glorifying, and feeling grateful to God. We glorify Him by saying *subhan Allah* (Glory be to God) by word and action in awareness of His Majesty. We exalt and magnify Him by saying *Allahu akbar* (God is the Greatest) through word and action in awareness of His Perfection. We offer thanks to Him by saying *al-hamdu lillah* (All praise be to God) with our heart, tongue, and body, in awareness of His Grace. From this, we conclude that the heart of prayer consists of glorification, exaltation, praise, and thanksgiving. Thus, these three phrases are present in all words and actions of those who pray. Further, following each prayer, they are repeated 33 times each to confirm and complete the prayer's objectives. The meaning of prayer is pronounced consecutively with these concise utterances.

SECOND POINT: We are God's servants. Aware of our defects, weakness, and poverty in the Divine presence, we prostrate in love and awe before His Lordship's perfection, His Divine Might on which every creature relies, and His

Divine Compassion. Just as His Lordship's sovereignty demands devotion and obedience, His Holiness requires us to see our defects and seek His pardon, to proclaim that He has no defect, that the false judgments of the ignorant are meaningless, and that He is beyond all failings of His creatures.

His Might's Perfection requires that, realizing our weakness and the helplessness of all creatures, we proclaim: "God is the Greatest" in admiration and amazement before the majesty of the Eternally Besought One's works. Bowing humbly, we are to seek refuge in Him and place our trust in Him. His Compassion's boundless treasury demands that we declare our need and those of all creatures by praying and asking for His help, and that we proclaim His blessings through praise and gratitude by uttering *al-hamdu lillah*. In short, the prayer's words and actions comprise all these meanings, and so were ordered and arranged by God.

THIRD POINT: Each person is a miniature of the universe. In the same way, the Qur'an's first *sura* (chapter), *Surat al-Fatiha*, is an illuminated miniature of the whole Book, and the prayer is a bright index involving all ways of worship, a sacred map hinting at the diverse kinds of worship practiced by all living entities.

FOURTH POINT: The consecutive divisions of day and night, as well as the years and phases of your life, function like a huge clock's wheels and levers. For example:

The time for *fajr* (before sunrise) may be likened to spring's birth, the moment when sperm takes refuge in the protective womb, or to the first of the 6 consecutive days during which Earth and the sky were created. It recalls how God disposes His Power and acts in such times and events.

The time for *zuhr* (just past midday) may be likened to the completion of adolescence, the middle of summer, or the period of humanity's creation in the world's lifetime. It points to God's compassionate manifestations and abundant blessings in those events and times. The time for *'asr* (afternoon) resembles autumn, old age, and the time of the Last Prophet (the Era of Happiness). It also calls to mind the Divine acts and the All-Compassionate's favors in them.

The time for *maghrib* (sunset) reminds us of many creatures' decline at the end of autumn and also of our own death. It thus forewarns us of the world's destruction at the Resurrection's beginning, teaches us how to understand the manifestation of God's Majesty, and wakes us from a deep sleep of neglect. The time for *'isha* (nightfall) calls to mind the world of darkness, veiling all daytime objects with its black shroud, and winter covering the dead Earth's surface with its white shroud. It brings to mind the remaining works of the dead being forgotten, and points to this testing arena's inevitable, complete decline. Thus *'isha* proclaims the awesome acts of the Overpowering One of Majesty.

Night reminds us of winter, the grave, the Inter-mediate World, and how much our spirit needs the All-Merciful One's Mercy. The late-night *tahajjud* prayer reminds and warns us of how necessary this prayer's light will be in the grave's darkness. By recalling the True Bestower's infinite bounties granted during these extraordinary events, it proclaims how worthy He is of praise and thanks.

The next morning points to the morning following the Resurrection. Just as morning follows night and spring comes after winter, so the morning of the Resurrection or "spring" follows the intermediate life.

Each appointed prayer time is the beginning of a vital turning point and a reminder of greater revolutions or turning points in the universe's life. Through the awesome daily disposals of the Eternally Besought One's Power, the prayer times remind us of the Divine Power's miracles and the Divine Mercy's gifts regardless of time or place. So the prescribed prayers, which are an innate duty, the basis of worship, and an unquestionable obligation, are most appropriate and fitted for these times.

FIFTH POINT: We are created weak, yet everything involves, affects, and saddens us. We have no power, yet are afflicted by calamities and enemies. We are extremely poor, yet have many needs. We are indolent and incapable, yet the burden of life is very heavy. Being human, we are connected with the rest of the world, yet what we love and are familiar with disappears, and the resulting grief causes us pain. Our mentality and senses inspire us toward glorious objectives and eternal gains, but we are unable, impatient, powerless, and have only a short lifetime.

Given all of this, several things become quite clear:

The *fajr* prayer is essential, for we must present a petition before the day's activities begin. Through prayer and supplication, we must beseech the Court of an All-Powerful One of Majesty, an All-Compassionate One of Grace, for success and help. Such support is necessary to bear and endure the troubles and burdens waiting for us.

The *zuhr* prayer is essential, for this is when the day starts to move forward to complete its course. People take a break from their activities. The spirit needs a pause from the heedlessness and insensibility caused by hard work, and Divine bounties are fully manifest. Praying at this time is good, necessary, agreeable, and proper. This prayer gives relief from the pressures of daily life and heedlessness. We stand humbly in the presence of the Real Bestower of blessings, express gratitude, and pray for His help. We bow to demonstrate helplessness before His Glory and Might, and prostrate to proclaim our wonder, love, and humility before His everlasting Perfection and matchless Grace.

The 'asr prayer resembles and recalls the sad season of autumn, the mournful state of old age, and the distressing period at the end of time. The day's tasks are brought toward completion, and the Divine bounties received that day (e.g., health, safety, and good service in His way) have accumulated to form a great total. It is also the time when the sun fades away, proving that everything is impermanent. We, who long for eternity, are created for it and show reverence for favors received, also are saddened by separations. So we stand up, perform *wudu'* (ablution), and pray.

Thus praying *'asr* is an exalted duty, an appropriate service, a reasonable way of paying a debt of gratitude, and an agreeable pleasure. We acquire peace of mind and find true consolation and ease of spirit by supplicating at the Eternal Court of the Everlasting, the Eternally Self-Subsistent One, and seeking refuge in His infinite Mercy, offering thanks and praise for His endless bounties, bowing humbly before His Lordship's Might and Glory, and prostrating humbly before His Eternal Divinity.

Evening reminds us of winter's beginning, the sad farewells of summer and autumn creatures, and our sorrowful separation from loved ones through death. The sun's lamp is extinguished, and Earth's inhabitants will emigrate to the other world following this one's destruction. It is also a severe warning for those who adore transient, ephemeral beloveds, each of whom will die.

By its nature, the human spirit longs for an Eternal Beauty. During this prayer, it turns toward the Eternal Being, Who creates and frames everything, Who commands huge heavenly bodies. At this time, the human spirit refuses to rely on anything finite and cries *Allahu akbar* (God is the Greatest). Then, in His presence, we say *al-hamdu lillah* (all praise be to God) to praise Him in the awareness of His faultless Perfection, matchless Beauty and Grace, and infinite Mercy.

Afterwards, by declaring: *You alone do we worship, and from You alone do We seek help* (1:5), we offer our worship of, and seek help from, His unassisted Lordship, unpartnered Divinity, and unshared Sovereignty. Bowing before His infinite Greatness, limitless Power, and perfect Honor and Glory, we demonstrate, with the rest of creation, our weakness and helplessness, humility and poverty by saying: "Glory be to my Lord, the

Mighty." Prostrating in awareness of the undying Beauty and Grace of His Essence, His unchanging sacred Attributes, and His constant everlasting Perfection, we proclaim, through detachment from all that is not Him, our love and servanthood in wonder and self-abasement. Finding an All-Beautiful Permanent, an All-Compassionate Eternal One to Whom we say: "Glory be to my Lord, the Most Exalted," we declare our Most Exalted Lord free of any decline or fault.

Then we sit reverently and willingly offer all creatures' praises and glorifications to the Eternal, All-Powerful, and All-Majestic One. We also ask God to bestow peace and blessings on His holy Messenger in order to renew our allegiance to him, proclaim our obedience to His commands, and renew and strengthen our belief. By viewing the universe's wise order, we testify to the Creator's Oneness and Muhammad's Messengership, herald of the sovereignty of God's Lordship, proclaimer of what pleases Him, and interpreter of the Book of the Universe's signs or verses.

Given this, how can we be truly human if we do not realize what the evening prayer represents:

an agreeable duty, a valuable and pleasurable service, a fine and beautiful worship, a serious matter, a significant conversation with the Creator, and a source of permanent happiness in this transient guest-house?

The time of *'isha* (nightfall), when night covers Earth, reminds us of the mighty disposals of God's Lordship as the Changer of Night and Day. It calls to our mind the Divine activities of the All-Wise One of Perfection as the Subduer of the sun and the moon, observed in His turning the white page of day into the black page of night, and in His changing summer's beautifully colored script into winter's frigid white page. It recalls His acts as the Creator of Life and Death in sending the dead entity's remaining works to another world. It reminds us of God's majestic control and graceful manifestations as the Creator of the Heavens and Earth, and that this narrow, mortal, and lowly world will be destroyed.

The same is true for the unfolding of the broad, eternal, and majestic world of the Hereafter. It also warns that only the One Who so easily turns day into night, winter into summer, and this world into the other world can be the universe's Owner and True Master. Only He is worthy to be worshipped and truly loved.

At nightfall our spirits, which are infinitely helpless and weak, infinitely poor and needy, tossed to and fro by circumstances and whirling onward into a dark and unknown future, perform the *'isha* prayer. We say, like Abraham: *I do not love those that set* (6:76). We seek refuge at the Court of the Ever-Living, the Ever-Worshipped, the Eternal Beloved One. From our transient life in this dark, fleeting world and dark future, we beseech the Enduring, Everlasting One. For a moment of unending conversation, a few seconds of immortal life, we seek the All-Merciful and Compassionate's favors. We ask for the light of His guidance that will illuminate our world and our future, and bind up the pain from the decline of all creatures and friends.

We forget the world, which has left us for the night, and pour out our heart's grief at the Court of Mercy. Before death-like sleep comes, after which anything can happen, we perform our "last" duty of worship. To close our day's activities on a favorable note, we pray and enter the Eternal Beloved and Worshipped One's presence, rather than the mortal ones we loved all day; the All-Powerful and Generous One's presence, rather than the impotent creatures from which we begged all day; and the All-Compassionate Protector's presence in the hope of being saved from the evil of the harmful creatures before which we trembled all day.

We start the prayer with *Surat al-Fatiha*, which extols praising the Lord of the worlds, Perfect and Self-Sufficient, Compassionate and All-Generous. We move on to *You alone do We worship* (1:5). That is, despite our insignificance and being alone, our connection with the Owner of the Day of Judgment, the Eternal Sovereign, causes us to be treated like an indulged guest and important officer. Through *You alone do we worship and from You alone do we seek help* (1:5), we offer Him the worship of all creatures and seek His assistance for them. Saying *Guide us to the Straight Path* (1:6), we ask to be guided to eternal happiness and the radiant way.

Saying *God is the Greatest*, we bow down and contemplate the Grandeur of the Majestic One, Who orders hidden suns and waking stars, that are like individual soldiers subject to His command just like the plants and animals that have now gone to sleep, and are His lamps and servants in this world.

We think of all creatures' universal prostration. That is, like the creatures that sleep at night, when all creation living in a certain age or period is discharged from the duty of worship by the command of *"Be!" and it is* like a well-ordered army of obedient soldiers, and is sent to the World of the Unseen, it prostrates on the rug of death in perfect orderliness saying: "God is the Greatest." They are resurrected in the spring by an arousing, life-giving trumpet-blast from the command of *Be! and it is*, and rise up to serve their Lord. Insignificant humanity makes the same declaration in the presence of the All-Merciful One of Perfection, the All-Compassionate One of Grace, in wonder-struck love, eternity-tinged humility, and dignified self-effacement. We then prostrate and achieve a sort of Ascension.

Thus each prescribed prayer time points to a mighty revolution, is a sign to the Master's tremendous activity, and a token of the universal Divine bounties. And so this matter is a result of perfect wisdom.

Glory be to You. We have no knowledge save what You have taught us. Truly, you are the All-Knowing, the All-Wise.

O God! Bestow blessings and peace upon the one You sent as a teacher to Your servants to instruct them in knowledge of You and worship of You; to make known the treasures of Your Names, the interpreter of the signs or verses of Your Book of the Universe; to serve as a mirror, through his worship, to the Grace of Your Lordship; and upon his Family and Companions. Have mercy on us and all believers. Amen. For the sake of Your Compassion, O Most Compassionate of the Compassionate.

THE ELEVENTH WORD

Creation and Prayer

In the Name of God,
the Merciful, the Compassionate.

> By the sun and its brightness, the moon when it follows it, the day when it reveals it, the night when it enshrouds it, heaven and He Who built it, Earth and He Who spread it, and the soul and Him Who perfected it. (91:1-7)

If you want to understand something of His purposes for creating humanity and the universe, and why the five daily prayers are obligatory, listen to this parable: A king had a vast treasury of precious stones and buried treasuries known only to him. He was well-versed in all industries, and had a vast knowledge of all artistic and scientific disciplines. As anyone who has beauty and perfection naturally tends to show them to others,[20] he

---
[20] Especially beauty and perfection that is admired by all and beneficial to others. (Tr.)

wanted to build a palace that would show his kingdom's magnificence, his wealth's splendor and extent, and the wonderful products of his artistry and skill. He also desired to behold his beauty and perfection with his own discerning eye and through the eyes of others.

And so he began to build a very large, magnificent palace. Dividing it into many apartments and rooms, he decorated it with his finest and most beautiful works of art, and embellished it with his precious stones. Designing it according to artistic and scientific principles and disciplines, he furnished it with the miraculous products of his knowledge. Finally, he prepared delicious specific foods and drinks for each family that would live therein, and provided them so elaborately, generously, and artistically that each food seem to be derived from at least 100 separate skills.

Then, the king settled some of his subjects in the palace. He sent his aide-de-camp to explain why he had built it, the rules they had to obey, what kind of being the king was, and about the palace's architecture, decorations, furniture, and ornaments. The king told his aide-de-camp to explain how the palace's structures, designs, and

Creation and Prayer

contents demonstrate his artistry and perfections, and how those dwelling in it can please him.

The aide-de-camp had many students, and each of his numerous assistants was deputed for a certain apartment. Standing among his students, he addressed the audience:

> O people! Our master, who owns this palace, built it to make himself known to you. In return, know and recognize him properly. He wants to make himself lovable to you through these ornaments. In return, appreciate his artistry and commend him for his works, thereby making yourselves loved by him. His favors demonstrate his love for you, so love him by obeying him. His offerings display his care and compassion for you, so thank him by showing your respect for him. Through the works of his perfection, the master wants to show his beauty and grace. In return, exhibit a great desire to see him and secure his attention. By setting his special stamp, which cannot be copied, on everything you see, he demonstrates that he is unique, absolutely independent and without partner, that this palace and its contents are his work and belong to him exclusively. So, acknowledge his uniqueness, absolute independence, and lack of partner.

The aide-de-camp continued his address. The palace's inhabitants were of two types. People in the first group, sensible and aware of themselves, saw the palace's wonders and concluded that everything had a purpose. While thinking about this, they listened to the aide-de-camp and learned what those purposes were. They did what the king wanted, and so pleased him. In return, the king invited them to a far larger and indescribably more beautiful palace, wherein he gave them all kinds of eternal bounties and blessings.

People in the second group were morally corrupt, unaware, and lacked sound reasoning. They only saw delicious food and did not understand the meaning behind the decorations and embellishments. Ignoring the address and directives of the aide-de-camp and his assistants, they focused on eating and sleeping. After drinking forbidden beverages, they became drunk, bothered the servants and guests, and broke the rules. So, the king imprisoned them.

In short, the glorious king built the palace for the purposes explained by his aide-de-camp. Realizing these purposes depends on two things. First, if the aide-de-camp did not exist, those purposes would be as nothing, for a book without a teacher to explain it is only a pack of sheets. Second, the aid-de-camp must be obeyed, for his existence is the reason for creating the palace, and its inhabitants' obedience is the reason for maintaining it. Without an aide-de-camp to make the palace known to its inhabitants and tell them of the king's will, the latter would not have built it. Also, if they ignore the king's instructions, the palace will be destroyed.

If you understand this, reflect upon its meaning. The palace is this world, whose roof is the heavens illuminated with smiling stars, whose floor is Earth's surface embellished with many kinds of flowers. The king is the Most Holy One, the Eternal King, Whom the seven firmaments and Earth, along with all their contents, glorify and extol in tongues specific to each. He is such a Powerful King that He created the heavens and Earth in 6 days.[21] Seated on His Throne of

---

[21] Like the Bible, the Qur'an mentions that God created the universe in 6 days. However, the Qur'an never mentions mornings and evenings, and presents "day" as a relative period whose measure is unknown. See 22:47, 32:5, and 70:4: (Tr.)

Lordship [that is, through His Lordship's continuous manifestations[22]], He alternates day and night like a white and a black thread, to inscribe His signs on the vast sheet of the universe. He is One, All-Majestic and Powerful, to Whom the sun, the moon, and the stars are all subjugated.

The palace's rooms are the thousands of worlds, each designed, furnished, and decorated in a specific way. The finest and most beautiful works of art are what we see here, each of which is a miracle of Divine Power; the foods are the wonderful fruits of Divine Mercy that we see here, especially in summer; and the kitchen is the fire in Earth's center and the sun's heat. The precious stones are manifestations of the Divine Sacred Names, and the embellishments are the well-ordered, finely made beings and perfectly proportioned inscriptions of the Pen of the Power that adorn this world and point to the Names of the Majestic All-Powerful One.

---

[22] The original word translated as "Lord" is Rabb. It denotes God as One Who brings up, trains, educates, sustains, and administers His creatures. Note: It must not be confused with the Christian understanding of "Lord," namely, Jesus Christ as the "Son of God." (Tr.)

The aide-de-camp is our master Prophet Muhammad. His assistants are all other Prophets, and his students are all saints and purified scholars. The servants are angels, the palace's inhabitants are jinn and humanity, and the invited guests are those animals created to serve humanity. The first group of people are believers, students of the Qur'an that interprets the verses of the Book of the Universe. The second group are the unbelievers and rebels, "deaf and dumb" misguided people who, obeying their carnal selves and Satan, accept only the worldly life and so place themselves below animals.

The first group, the good and spiritually prosperous people, listened to the master's message of intellectual enlightenment and spiritual well-being, the path of prosperity in both worlds. That master is a worshipping servant in regard to servanthood, who describes his Master and makes Him known to people; his community's envoy in Almighty God's court; and a Messenger in regard to Messengership, who communicates his Master's commandments to humanity and jinn via the Qur'an.

These people found themselves in elevated stations and invested with many subtle and pleasing duties of the prescribed prayer, the index of all varieties of worship:

- **FIRST:** They saw the Divine works and, seeing themselves in the station of objective observers of the Kingdom of Divine Lordship's wonders, said "God is the Greatest" while glorifying and extolling Him.

- **SECOND:** Seeing themselves in the station of announcing the Divine Sacred Names' precious manifestations, they praised and esteemed Him as the All-Holy via these words: "Glory be to God. All praise be to God."

- **THIRD:** In the station of tasting and perceiving (with their outer and inner senses) the bounties stored in Divine Mercy's treasuries, they gave thanks and praised Him.

- **FOURTH:** In the station of weighing the jewels in the Divine Names' treasuries with the scales of their mental and spiritual faculties, they praised and declared God to be without fault.

- **FIFTH:** In the station of studying the Master's Messages written on the lines of Destiny by the Pen of His Power, they contemplated and commended Him.

- **SIXTH:** In the station of observing the subtle beauties and delicacies in the creation of things, as well as in the art of creation and declaring God to be without fault, they set out to fulfil their duty of loving and yearning for their Majestic Originator and Gracious Maker.

Therefore, while observing the universe and its contents, they addressed God indirectly and did all duties of worship in the stations mentioned above. Then, seeing the Wise Maker's actions and the way He acts, they were amazed by the realization of how the Majestic Creator makes Himself known to conscious beings through the miracles of His art.

In direct response, they proclaimed in His presence: "Glory be to You. We cannot know You as required by Your knowledge—as the duty of knowing You requires. What makes You known are Your miracles displayed in Your creatures." In response to the All-Merciful making Himself loved through the lovely fruits of His Mercy, they proclaimed in love and ecstasy: *You alone do we worship, and from You alone do we seek help* (1:5). In response to the Real Giver of

Bounties exhibiting His Care and Compassion through His decorous gifts, they thanked and praised Him, saying: "Glory be to You, and all praise be to You." In other words:

> You are so worthy of thanks and praise that all Your favors in the universe praise You in the tongue of their disposition. All Your bounties arranged and exhibited in the world's market and on Earth's face declare Your praise and commendation. The beautiful, well-proportioned fruits and produce of Your Mercy and Graciousness on Earth in due measure and quantity bear witness to Your Generosity and Magnificence, and thereby thank You before the eyes of all creatures.

In response to His displaying His Grace, Majesty, Perfection, and Grandeur in the "mirrors" of creatures constantly recruited and renewed, they stated: "God is the Greatest," and bowed before Him in due perception of their own impotence. Afterward, they prostrated in humility and with wonder and love. Then, before the All-Wealthy One's display of His Wealth's abundance and His Mercy's comprehensiveness, they showed their poverty and need by praying: *From You alone do we seek help* (1:5).

In response to the Majestic Maker's exhibition of His art's subtlety and wonder through animate beings, they showed their appreciation by saying: "What (wonders) God has willed," and their commendation by saying: "How beautifully they have been made." Continuing to observe, they said: "God bless them. How wonderfully they have been made," and testified to Him by proclaiming their belief. In full admiration, they called everyone to witness the same: "Come and see! Attach yourselves to the way to prosperity!"

In response to the Eternal King's declaration of His Lordship's Kingdom and His Oneness' manifestation throughout the universe, they believed in and confirmed His Unity, and showed their obedience and submission by saying: "We have heard and obeyed." To the manifestation of the Lord of the Worlds' Divinity, they responded with worship by declaring their impotence embedded in weakness, their poverty embedded in need, and the prescribed prayer (the essence of worship).

While in that huge mosque of the world, they devoted themselves to these and similar duties of worship and so assumed the best pattern of creation. Above all other creatures, they became

God's trustworthy vicegerents, equipped with the blessing of belief and trustworthiness.[23] After this trial and testing, and to recompense their devotion to Islam, their Munificent Lord rewarded their belief with eternal happiness and invited them to the Abode of Peace.

There, out of His Mercy, He bestowed on them dazzling bounties beyond description and imagination, and eternity and everlasting life. The observing and reflecting lovers of an eternal, abiding beauty will go to eternity. Such is the end and final station of the Qur'an's students. May Almighty God include us among them. Amen!

Members of the second group, all of them sinners and wicked people, entered the palace of this world at the age of discretion.[24] Disbelieving the evidence of Divine Oneness and ungrateful for the bounties, they insulted all creatures by accusing them of being worthless, and rejected and denied the Divine Names' manifestations. In sum,

---

[23] God's vicegerency is defined as humanity being the "means" used by God to execute His commands on Earth and ruling on it according to His laws. (Tr.)

[24] Islam considers a person to have reached the "age of discretion" when he or she becomes physically mature.

they committed an infinite error in a short time and deserved eternal punishment.

We have been given this capital of life and human faculties to spend on the duties mentioned above. Given this, our duty is not restricted to living an easy life (according to the requisites of modern corrupt civilization) and gratifying our carnal desires. Nor are our delicate senses and abilities, sensitive faculties and organs, well-ordered members and systems, and inquisitive senses and feelings included in the "machine" of our life (our body) to satisfy the base, carnal self's low desires.

Rather, they were included therein and made a part of our nature for two reasons: First, to make us feel all varieties of the bounties bestowed by the Real Giver of Bounties, and to urge us to be grateful. So, feel them and be grateful to Him. Second, to make known and urge us to experience all manifestations of each Divine Sacred Name seen in the universe. So experience and know them, and believe. If we can realize these aims, we can gain human perfection and become true human beings.

As shown in the following parable, we were not given our human faculties only to earn our worldly sustenance: A master gave a servant 20 gold coins and told him to buy a suit of a particular cloth. The servant bought and then wore a fine suit made from the best quality of cloth. The master gave another servant 1,000 gold coins, put a written list in his pocket, and sent him to do some trade. Obviously the money was not to be used for clothes. So if the second servant did not read the list, but rather chose to imitate the other servant by buying a suit with the money given to him, and, moreover, received a suit of the worst possible quality, would not his master reprimand and punish him severely for his stupidity?

O my carnal self and my friend! You are not sent here to spend your life's capital and your vital potentials on material pleasures and this transient life. If you do, you will fall to the lowest ranks, although you are far superior with regard to "capital" than the most developed animal.

O my heedless self! If you want some understanding of your life's aim and nature, apparent form and meaning, and the perfect happiness in your life, weigh on the scales of your body's senses the bounties stored in Divine Mercy's treasuries and offer thanks on your body's behalf. Through the feelings, tendencies, and faculties embedded in your nature, discover the hidden treasuries—the works and manifestations—of the Divine Sacred Names and then recognize the Most Holy One through those Names.

In this place of exhibition, consciously display through your life the Divine Names' subtle manifestations in your being [such as your senses, faculties, and abilities] before all creation. Proclaim your worship and servanthood to the Court of the Creator's Lordship, verbally and through the tongue of your disposition. In the manner of a soldier who, appearing before the king with the decorations received from him, displays the marks of the king's favor, consciously adorn yourself with the "jewels" of subtle human senses and faculties embedded in your being through the Divine Names' manifestations and present yourself before the Eternal Witness.

Other living beings worship and glorify their Creator by consciously or unconsciously obeying the laws He established for their lives. This is the main purpose for their creation and life. Thus you should consciously observe their obedience to Him, their worship and glorification of Him, and reflect on and testify to these deeds.

Using your defective attributes (e.g., partial knowledge, power, and will) as units of measurement, recognize the Majestic Creator's absolute Attributes and sacred Qualities. For example, you can build a beautiful and well-ordered house by using your limited attributes, so understand that the Maker of this palace of the universe is far more powerful, wise, and capable. As for the Creator's Oneness and the Maker's Lordship, you can and should perceive how each being proclaims them in its own language. From your impotence and weakness, poverty and need, infer the degrees of the Divine Power's manifestations and the Master's Richness. Just as food's pleasures and varieties are understood or distinguished according to your hunger and need, understand the degrees of infinite Divine Power and Richness through your infinite impotence and poverty.

Briefly, those are the aims of your life, the nature of which can be summarized as follows: It is an index of wonders originating in the Divine Names, a measure to consider the Divine Attributes, a unit to know the worlds in the universe, a catalogue of the macrocosm, a map of the universe and its fruit or compressed form, a set of keys with which to open Divine Power's hidden treasuries, and a most excellent pattern of the Divine perfections reflected in creatures and manifested through time.

The following describes the apparent, observable form of your life and its meaning: Your life is an inscribed word, a wisdom-displaying word written by the Pen of Power. Observed and sensed, it points to the Divine Beautiful Names. Your life's meaning is to be a mirror to reflect the Divine manifestation of Divine Oneness and the Divine manifestation as the Eternally-Besought-of-All. Through its comprehensiveness as the focal point for all Divine Names shown in the world, it functions as a mirror to reflect the Single and Eternally Besought One.

As for the perfection of your life in happiness, it is to perceive and love the lights of the Eternal Sun pictured in the mirror of your life, to display ardor for Him as a conscious being, to be enraptured with love of Him, and to establish His Light's reflection in the center of your heart. As a result of all this, a *hadith qudsi* expresses your rank among the highest ranks by saying: "(God said): I am not contained in the heavens and Earth, but I am contained in the believer's heart."

So, my selfhood! Your life was given to you so that you could realize such sublime aims. As you have the potential to acquire such priceless treasures, how can you even think of wasting it on gratifying fleeting carnal desires and seeking transient worldly pleasures? So as not to waste it, reflect on the oaths and the following truths in the verses below and act accordingly:

> By the sun and its morning brightness; by the moon when it follows it; by the day when it reveals it; by the night when it enshrouds it; by heaven and He Who built it; by Earth and He Who spread it; by the soul and Him Who perfected it, and inspired it (with conscience) of what is wrong for it and what is right for it. He is indeed prosperous who purifies it, and he has indeed failed who corrupts it. (91:1-10)

> O God! Bestow blessings and peace on the sun of the sky of Messengership, on the moon of the constellation of Prophethood, and on his Family and Companions, who are the stars of guidance. Have mercy upon us and all believers. Amen! Amen! Amen!

THE TWENTY-FIRST WORD

The Prayer

(Note: This Word consists of two stations. In this book, only the first station is included.)

In the name of God,
the Merciful, the Compassionate.

First station

Consider the following verse:

> Surely the prayer is a timed prescription for believers. (4:103)

Once a well-known and socially important old man said to me: "Prayer is okay, but five times a day is too much; it bores and wearies." A long time after this, my carnal soul told me the same thing. I realized that its laziness had caused it to listen to this satanic idea. Understanding that those words had been spoken in the name of all evil-commanding souls, I told myself: "Since my soul orders evil, and one who does not reform his own soul cannot reform others, I shall begin with my own soul." I said: "O soul. In response to such ignorant words said in the bed of indolence and the torpor of idleness, I relay five warnings."

FIRST WARNING: O wretched soul. Is your life permanent? Are you sure that you will be here next year or even tomorrow? Your weariness comes from your fancy that you will live forever. You complain as though you will remain here forever in eternal enjoyment. If only you understood that your life is short and passes in vain, you would understand that prayer, far from causing boredom or weariness, is rather a fine, agreeable, easy, and gracious act of service; that it is the means to happiness in the real, eternal life; and that it actually arouses vigor and gives pleasure.

SECOND WARNING: O gluttonous soul. Every day you eat, drink and breathe. Yet this does not bore you, for these needs recur and so give pleasure when satisfied. Thus the five daily prayers should not bore you, for they attract and conduct the necessary sustenance, water of life, and air to your body's parts (e.g., your heart, spirit, and inward spiritual faculties).

The food and strength of a heart exposed to endless grief and pain, and inclined to infinite pleasure and ambition, may be obtained by knocking on the One All-Compassionate and Munificent's door. For a spirit connected with most beings and moving quickly to the other world amid cries of separation, the water of life may be imbibed by turning, through the five daily prayers, toward the Everlasting Beloved's spring. A conscious inward sense, a luminous spiritual faculty, by nature desires the eternity for which it was created. As an infinitely delicate and subtle mirror to the Eternal Being, it is most needy of "air," of relief and relaxation, so that it can deal success-fully with the distressing, crushing, and suffocating conditions of worldly life. It can "breathe" only through the "window" of prayer.

THIRD WARNING: O impatient soul. Why do you think of the hardship of past worship, the difficulties of praying, of troubles and calamities? Why are you distressed? Why do you anticipate the difficulties of future worship and service in prayer, and the pain of future misfortune? Why are you impatient? You are like a foolish commander who, upon seeing one flank of enemy forces join the right flank and thus reinforce it, sends a significant part of his center forces there. This only weakens his own center. Also, although no enemy forces are attacking the left flank, he sends a large contingent there and tells it to fire, thereby greatly weakens his own center. This encourages the enemy to attack the center and rout the troops.

Moreover, past troubles are now a mercy. Their pain has gone, while their pleasure remains. Hardships have changed into blessings, and trials and toils into rewards. So why should you be weary? Rather, feel a new eagerness and a fresh zeal, and make a serious effort to continue. Why should you worry about the future, which has not yet come? This is as ridiculous as complaining now about future hunger and thirst, of thinking of them now and feeling bored and wearied. Since this is the truth, consider only today when it comes to matters of worship. Say: "I am spending 1 hour out of 24 on pleasant and elevated acts of service, the reward for which is great and whose trouble is little." Your bitter disappointment will change into a pleasurable endeavor.

O impatient soul. You are charged with three types of perseverance: worship, refraining from sin, and enduring misfortune. Allow yourself to be guided by the truth contained in the third warning, and call: "O Most Persevering One." Derive strength from these three types of perseverance. Using your God-given power of perseverance in the proper way will suffice for every difficulty and misfortune, so hold on with that power.

FOURTH WARNING: O foolish soul. Is this duty of worship so fruitless and its reward so little that you feel weary? Consider this: If someone offers you money or threatens you, you would work until evening without respite.

Are the five daily prayers in vain? Are they not your weak heart's "food" in this guest-house of the world, sustenance and light in your grave (a station to eternal life), a document and warrant on the Day of Judgment, and a light and a mount on the Bridge that everyone has to cross? Is their reward so little? If someone promised you an expensive present, you would work for several days. Though he may go back on his word, you would trust him and work without any respite.

Consider the following case. One Who never breaks His promise says that He will reward you with something like Paradise and a gift like eternal happiness. He employs you for a very short time in a most agreeable duty. If you leave that service undone, act in a manner to accuse Him of His promise, or belittle His gift by working reluctantly as if being forced, would you not deserve a severe reprimand and a terrible punishment? While you work without slacking at the most difficult jobs in this world out of your fear of imprisonment, you do not fear an eternal imprisonment like Hell or show any zeal for so light and pleasant an act of service as the prayers. How do you explain this?

FIFTH WARNING: O worldly minded soul. Are your sluggishness in worship and deficiency in the prescribed five daily prayers due to your many worldly preoccupations? Are you pressed for time on account of the struggle for livelihood? Were you created only for this world? Is it reasonable to spend all your time on it?

Your potential makes you superior to all animals. But even a sparrow can do a better job than you when it comes to satisfying your daily needs. Your duty as a human being is to work for the real, everlasting life. You are not an animal! Most worldly concerns are trivial and useless matters from which you derive no benefit. And yet, leaving aside the most essential things, you spend your time acquiring useless information, as if you had thousands of years to live. For example, why do you wonder about Saturn's rings, or how many chickens there are in America? Are you preparing a doctorate in astronomy or in livestock statistics?

If you say: "The essential requirements of earning a livelihood keep me from the prayer and make me tired," my answer will be: Suppose that you work for a daily wage of a dollar, and someone comes and tells you: "Dig here for 10 minutes, and you'll find a brilliant emerald worth $100." If you reply: "No, I won't come, because the boss will cut my wage by 10 cents, and so I will earn less," you can see how foolish that argument is. Or, you work in your orchard for your livelihood.

If you abandon the prescribed prayers, all the fruits of your work are limited to a worldly, insignificant, and unproductive livelihood. However, if you pray during your rest periods, your spirit will become lively and your heart will experience ease. You also will discover two mines, both of which are important sources for a productive worldly livelihood and for your provisions for the Hereafter: First, through a sound intention, you will receive a share in the glorifications offered by your orchard's plants and trees.

Second, whatever produce is eaten, by people or animals, will return to you like alms. But this will happen only if you work in the Real Provider's name and within His permission's sphere, and consider yourself a distribution official distributing His property among His creatures.

See what a great loss you will experience if you do not pray, what significant wealth you will lose, and how you will be deprived of the two mines that support your efforts with high motives and actions with strong morale. As you age, you will grow weary of gardening and saying: "What's all this to me? I'm leaving the world anyway, so why bother?" slide into idleness. But those who pray and work for their livelihood say: "I shall try harder to perform the obligatory worship and earn legitimately and honestly so that I may send more light to my grave and procure more provisions for my life in the Hereafter."

In short: O soul, yesterday has left you and you have no guarantee that you will be alive tomorrow. Your life consists of today. Set at least one hour aside for the mosque or the prayer mat, a savings box and reserve fund for the Hereafter. Set this hour aside for your real future. Each new day is the door to a new world. If you do not pray, your world of that day will go dark and wretched and will testify against you in the World of Symbols, wherein the immaterial, essential forms of beings reside.

Each day, everyone has a private world, the nature of which depends on one's heart and deeds, contained in this world. Just as a magnificent palace reflected in a mirror assumes the mirror's color and quality, just as an uneven mirror shows the finest things to be coarse, so do you change your own world's appearance through your heart, mind, deeds, and attitudes. You may cause it either to testify for or against you.

If you pray and turn toward the All-Majestic Maker, your private world will be illuminated suddenly. Prayer resembles a powerful electric light switched on by your intention to pray. It disperses your world's darkness and shows that the changes and movements in this confused, tumultuous world arise from, and for the purpose of, a wise order and a meaningful arrangement of Divine Power. It disperses over your heart a light from the light-filled verse: *God is the Light of the heavens and Earth* (24:35). And, illuminating your world on that day through its reflection, that light will cause your world to testify for you through its luminosity.

Never say: "My prayers mean almost nothing when compared with the reality of what prayer should be." Just as the date-palm stone encapsulates and contains the tree itself (the difference is only between the summary and the fully evolved or elaborated form), a great saint's prayer is fully evolved while that of ordinary people like us (even if we are unaware of it) has a share in that Divine light. Even if you are not conscious of it, there is a mystery in this truth. However, our perception of and illumination by that truth varies according to our degrees.

Just as there are many stages and degrees between a date-palm's stone and the fully grown tree, praying and benefiting from our prayers are characterized by possibly even more numerous degrees and stages. However, the basis of that luminous truth is present in each degree or stage.

> O God. Bestow blessings and peace on him who said: "The prescribed prayers are the pillar of religion," and on his Family and Companions.

Index

A

Abraham (Prophet), 6, 77
angels, 34, 56, 87
animals, 6, 9, 14, 27, 38, 47, 79, 87, 104, 106
Arabic, 4, 19
Ascension, 79

B

Beauty (Divine), 56, 74, 75
belief, 19, 25, 28, 31, 32, 46, 49, 52, 55, 57, 63, 64, 65, 75, 91, 92
Bible, 85
Book of the Universe, 45, 75, 80, 87

C

carnal self, 46, 93, 94
cause, 15, 107, 108
chance, 35
civilization, 63, 93
Companions, 1, 24, 56, 65, 80, 98, 108
compassion, 9, 13, 14, 53, 83
conscience, 46, 98
contentment, 25, 53
contingent, 102
creation, 15, 17, 21, 38, 41, 45, 55, 69, 74, 79, 89, 91, 95

D

Day of Judgment, 78, 103
Day of Resurrection, 52
death, 26, 27, 51, 52, 55, 63, 64, 70, 74, 79
desire, 30, 48, 61, 63, 83
despair, 50
Destiny, 88
destruction, 29, 45, 70, 74
dissipation, 29, 42

E

enjoyment, 27, 50, 100
enlightenment, 87
eternal life, 34, 35, 52, 65, 100, 103
eternity, 11, 12, 22, 42, 73, 92, 101
evil, 31, 59, 61, 63, 78, 100
evil-commanding self, 59
Existence (Divine), 57

F

fear, 4, 5, 30, 39, 53, 104
forgiveness, 48
free will, 32, 38
freedom, 58, 61
future, 44, 77, 101, 102, 107

G

generosity, 64
goodness, 13, 14, 62
grace, 9, 12, 20, 83
gratitude, 13, 49, 68, 72, 73
grave, 30, 34, 49, 52, 54, 55, 63, 64, 70, 103, 106
guidance, 39, 55, 63, 77, 98

H

happiness, 25, 32, 42, 44, 49, 57, 64, 65, 76, 78, 92, 94, 97, 100, 103
harmony, 9, 22
heart, 8, 16, 17, 18, 26, 30, 43, 59, 63, 67, 77, 97, 100, 103, 105, 107
heavens, 17, 85, 97, 107
heedlessness, 72
Hell, 28, 32, 46, 47, 64, 65, 104
Hereafter, 30, 39, 47, 49, 52, 63, 76, 105, 106
humility, 72, 74, 79, 90

I

imagination, 32, 34, 43, 92
immortal, 77
impotence, 21, 46, 51, 55, 90, 91, 96
intention, 35, 62, 105, 107

J

Jesus (Prophet), 86
jinn, 27, 87
jurisprudence, 16

K

knowledge, 19, 24, 39, 61, 80, 81, 82, 89, 96

L

law, 5, 16, 48, 57, 59, 62
life, 6, 11, 14, 16, 23, 35, 37, 38, 39, 42, 43, 47, 49, 52, 63, 64, 65, 69, 71, 72, 77, 87, 92, 93, 94, 95, 96, 97, 100, 104, 106
light, 8, 9, 10, 11, 15, 18, 20, 22, 48, 49, 54, 55, 70, 77, 103, 104, 106, 107, 108
Lordship (Divine), 9, 14, 20, 56, 67, 73, 74, 75, 76, 80, 86, 88, 91, 95, 96
love, 12, 19, 42, 60, 67, 71, 72, 75, 77, 79, 83, 89, 90, 97

M

matter, 37, 76, 79
mercy, 21, 23, 24, 31, 53, 55, 56, 62, 65, 80, 98, 102
Messengership, 75, 87, 98
mind, 8, 14, 17, 18, 35, 52, 69, 70, 73, 76, 107
miracle, 10, 38, 86
misfortune, 46, 101, 102
Moses (Prophet), 6

N

nature, 9, 11, 15, 19, 36, 39, 46, 57, 62, 74, 93, 94, 96, 101, 107

O

obedience, 22, 32, 68, 75, 85, 91, 95
order, 4, 5, 14, 45, 58, 75, 107

P

Paradise, 28, 32, 40, 43, 44, 46, 47, 63, 64, 103
partners, 49
past, 1, 44, 69, 101, 102
patience, 52
Pharaoh, 42
philosophy, 54
piety, 30
pity, 61
pleasure, 25, 27, 53, 62, 73, 100, 102
poverty, 4, 5, 47, 51, 54, 55, 67, 74, 90, 91, 96
prayer, 23, 29, 34, 66, 67, 68, 70, 71, 72, 74, 75, 77, 78, 79, 88, 91, 99, 100, 101, 105, 106, 108
property, 40, 41, 42, 43, 47, 49, 106
Prophethood, 98
Prophets, 56, 87
punishment, 42, 49, 93, 104
purpose, 12, 60, 84, 95, 107

Q

R

reality, 30, 41, 51, 62, 63, 108
reason, 27, 59, 85
rebellion, 37, 63
reflection, 7, 97, 108
religion, 57, 108
Resurrection, 70
reward, 32, 46, 102, 103

S

saints, 87, 108
salvation, 38, 65
Satan, 37, 87
season, 73
security, 57
self, 36, 37, 44, 45, 47, 62, 94
self-effacement, 79
selfhood, 98
separation, 27, 47, 51, 52, 74, 101
servanthood, 75, 87, 95
service, 13, 61, 73, 76, 100, 101, 102, 104
sin, 47, 48, 102
Solomon (Prophet), 9
soul, 4, 8, 25, 27, 30, 34, 35, 37, 39, 43, 61, 81, 98, 99, 100, 101, 102, 103, 104, 106
spirit, 8, 17, 34, 38, 43, 44, 57, 59, 70, 72, 73, 74, 100, 105
Straight Path, 78

submission, 91
Sunna, 23

T

transgression, 32
transience, 47

U

ugliness, 47
unbelief, 27, 28, 32, 63
Unity (Divine), 10, 11, 16, 17, 21, 57, 91

V

vicegerency, 92
virtue, 63

W

weakness, 4, 5, 53, 67, 68, 74, 91, 96
willpower, 42
wisdom, 14, 17, 20, 79
worship, 16, 17, 18, 29, 30, 32, 35, 39, 69, 71, 74, 76, 77, 78, 79, 80, 88, 89, 91, 95, 101, 102, 103, 104, 106

X

Y

Z